Pebbles *of* WISDOM

Other Books from Jossey-Bass by Rabbi Adin Steinsaltz

The Miracle of the Seventh Day: A Guide to the Spiritual Meaning, Significance, and Weekly Practice of the Jewish Sabbath (2003)

Opening the Tanya: Discovering the Moral and Mystical Teachings of a Classic Work of Kabbalah (2003)

Learning from the Tanya: Volume Two in the Definitive Commentary on the Moral and Mystical Teachings of a Classic Work of Kabbalah (2005)

We Jews: Who Are We and What Should We Do? (2005)

Understanding the Tanya: Volume Three in the Definitive Commentary on a Classic Work of Kabbalah by the World's Foremost Authority (2007)

Other Books from Jossey-Bass by Arthur Kurzweil

Best Jewish Writing 2003

From Generation to Generation: How to Trace Your Jewish Genealogy and Family History (2004)

On the Road with Rabbi Steinsaltz: 25 Years of Pre-Dawn Car Trips, Mind-Blowing Encounters, and Inspiring Conversations with a Man of Wisdom (2006)

Pebbles *of* WISDOM

from Rabbi Adin Steinsaltz

COLLECTED and with NOTES by

Arthur Kurzweil

JOSSEY-BASS
A Wiley Imprint
www.josseybass.com

Published by Jossey-Bass
A Wiley Imprint
989 Market Street, San Francisco, CA 94103-1741—www.josseybass.com

Library of Congress Cataloging-in-Publication Data
Kurzweil, Arthur.
Pebbles of wisdom from Rabbi Adin Steinsaltz / Arthur Kurzweil, Adin Steinsaltz.
p. cm.
Includes bibliographical references and index.
ISBN 978-0-470-48592-7 (cloth)
1. Steinsaltz, Adin—Teachings. 2. Spiritual life—Judaism. 3. Jewish way of life.
I. Steinsaltz, Adin. II. Title.
BM755.S6915K88 2009
296.7—dc22
2009015720

Printed in the United States of America
FIRST EDITION
HB Printing 10 9 8 7 6 5 4 3 2 1

To

Rabbi Adin Steinsaltz

With love and devotion

ARTHUR KURZWEIL

CONTENTS

PART III The Children of Israel 105

PART IV Torah 135

PART V The Trials of Life 171

PART VI Guidance 201

ACKNOWLEDGMENTS

It has been thirty years since I began gathering these pebbles. And just about every person in my life knows that in virtually every conversation I have, I share a pebble of wisdom I have learned from Rabbi Steinsaltz. When a person shares the wisdom of his teacher, the light of that wisdom reflects back and forth, like a ribbon of light that connects two points.

I have had the privilege of sharing Rabbi Steinsaltz's teachings with many people, but special thanks are due to the following individuals, each of whom was truly a part of this gathering of pebbles from Rabbi Steinsaltz:

Bobby Kurzweil, my wife, partner, friend, *chevrusa,* editor, and inspiration.

Margy-Ruth Davis, for your friendship, your leadership, and your exceptional dedication to Rabbi Steinsaltz and his work.

Ruth Friedman, for your commitment to Rabbi Steinsaltz and your gentle kindness.

Jeff Burt, for your talents, modest generosity, and devotion to Rabbi Steinsaltz.

Meni Even-Israel, Thomas Nisell, Emanuel Quint, Chaim Billet, Meir Hanegbi, Yehudit Shabta, Jonathan Omer-man, Steve Shaw, and Meyer Weitz, for all of the ways you know you have helped and encouraged me and for ways you probably don't.

Yehuda Hanegbi, of blessed memory, for the gifts you were given by the Almighty and for the gifts you gave to the world.

Alan Rinzler, for your vision, your spirit, your loyalty, and most of all your friendship.

Paul Foster, for your generosity and encouragement.

Andrea Flint, for your talents, intuition, patience, and kindness.

Nana Twumasi for your talents and generous assistance.

Rebecca Allen, Muriel Jorgensen, and Bruce Emmer, for your editorial talents and consistent excellence.

Ken Kurzweil, for your endless patience, support, and so much more.

Saul and Evelyn Kurzweil, for showing me, since childhood, how to collect pebbles of wisdom.

Miriam Kurzweil, for your extraordinary spirit, your amazing insight and intuition, and the love you inspire. And for helping me with this gathering of pebbles.

Moshe Kurzweil, for your inspiring curiosity, your spirit, your leadership qualities, and for always being a *mensch.*

Malya Kurzweil, for your dazzling intelligence, your hysterical wit, and all of your exceptional ways.

Helen Hecht, for your care, your counsel, and your love.

So many people in their own particular ways have helped me gather these pebbles of wisdom. I feel particular gratitude as I express my thanks to:

Gary Eisenberg, Richard Carlow, Rick Blum, Marc Felix, Ed Rothfarb, Robin Bauer, Zsuzsa Barta, Alison Bermant, Robin Reingold, Diane Bloomfield, Marcia Cohen, Alan Kay, Jo Kay, Nathan Zimmerman, Susanne Hedaya, Ken Cohen, and Danny Siegel.

Blessed are You, Lord our God, Ruler of the Universe, who has kept us alive, sustained us, and permitted us to reach this moment.

Great Neck, New York
Pesach 2009

Arthur Kurzweil

INTRODUCTION

When I meet a person who learns that I am a serious student of the teachings of Rabbi Adin Steinsaltz of Jerusalem, I am usually asked to say something about him.

Sometimes I say, "Rabbi Steinsaltz was brought up in a secular home. His parents were secular leftists, and he says that he read Marx and Lenin before he read the Bible. His parents were skeptics and raised him to be a skeptic. Rabbi Steinsaltz once said, 'I'm such a skeptic that I became skeptical of skepticism.' "

Or I say, "Rabbi Steinsaltz is a brilliant and renowned Orthodox rabbi, destined to be one of the most important Jewish scholars in history. In one of his books, Rabbi Steinsaltz writes, 'If you think you've arrived, you're lost.'"

And at other times I say, "Rabbi Steinsaltz has done something that has not been done in one thousand years. It is not since the great biblical and Talmudic commentator Rashi that any one single individual has written and published a comprehensive commentary on the entire Talmud. And it is considered a masterpiece and a work of genius by people who are experts. His motto is 'Let my people know.' "

The first time I heard Rabbi Steinsaltz address an audience, in the early 1980s, I recorded it. During that talk, Rabbi Steinsaltz said, among other things, "Although I am a rabbi, I have avoided official positions like the plague. My only official position for many years was that I was on the board of the local zoo in Jerusalem."

And he said, "Many people come to me to talk privately, and many of these conversations are confessions of sins. So I have heard lots of confessions. I have to tell you that people haven't invented a new sin in the last three thousand years. Sometimes you wish to hear some new combination, some new idea. But you never find it."

He also said, "I grew up in a family where neither my mother nor my father went to synagogue. Not even on Yom Kippur. My father said that he did not go because he had too much respect for the place. He said—and I completely agree with him—that the synagogue is not a theater. Either you are a participant, or you don't go there. Because he could not be a participant, he would not go to watch."

And then he said, "My father was not particular about eating kosher when he was in Israel. But whenever he was abroad, he always ate kosher just for everyone to see. He was proud of being a Jew and of Jewish knowledge. When I was ten years old, my father hired a tutor to teach me Talmud. My father said, 'I don't mind if you're an atheist, but I don't want any member of my family to be an ignoramus. It is a shame for a Jew to be an ignoramus. Perhaps it is the lowest of the low that a Jew can reach. It means he lacks some essential knowledge about himself. Imagine that a person does not know that he has a head until he is sixty-five and that he discovered it accidentally. That is the kind of feeling that results from a Jew being ignorant."

A number of times over the years I have mentioned to Rabbi Steinsaltz that in his lectures, interviews, and writings, there are always such wonderful "gems" embedded within the transcripts and essays, and I find myself repeating these "gems" to people.

"Perhaps not 'gems,'" he responds. "Maybe pebbles."

So for nearly thirty years, I have been collecting pebbles from Rabbi Steinsaltz.

The metaphor works. A pebble can contain a gem. A pebble might be tiny but can be of great value. A pebble, used properly, can be quite effective. David killed Goliath with a pebble. The *Zohar* says that David had originally put five pebbles into his bag but that they miraculously became one.

The pebbles in Parts I through VI of this book are all from unpublished sources. In the Notes section, I have collected additional pebbles from published sources that relate to the unpublished ones. I have done this for two reasons: (1) to offer more pebbles to the reader and (2) to send the reader to Rabbi Steinsaltz's published works to see how the ideas in the pebbles are expanded—and then to discover even more pebbles, as well as lengthier pieces and more fully developed ideas.

The Notes section draws heavily on Rabbi Steinsaltz's book *The Thirteen Petalled Rose*. I predict that in addition to Rabbi Steinsaltz's Talmud translation and commentary, *The Thirteen Petalled Rose* will live forever by taking its place among the most important books of Jewish thought and theology ever published. Already a classic, *The Thirteen Petalled Rose* is one of those books that people report has changed their lives.

The pebbles in this book were found in the following places:

- **Conversations.** Over the years, I estimate that I have had over one hundred conversations with Rabbi Steinsaltz. Sometimes I recorded the conversations and transcribed them, but most of the time I made it my business, as soon as I left a conversation, to call one or more of my children and tell them every detail. The habit of repeating the stories and ideas that Rabbi Steinsaltz has told me over and over, combined with an excellent, sometimes photographic memory that God has given me, has allowed me to retain a large amount of Rabbi Steinsaltz's best pebbles. I have also sat in on some conversations Rabbi Steinsaltz had with others, and these conversations also became a part of the material available for this book.

- **Rabbi Steve Shaw.** Steve was instrumental in helping Rabbi Steinsaltz launch his publishing and teaching activities in the United States more than thirty years ago. In fact, Steve arranged my first meeting with Rabbi Steinsaltz in 1982. Steve told me that for a number of years when he hosted Rabbi Steinsaltz and arranged for his lectures, he recorded them. He also taped lengthy conversations between himself and Rabbi Steinsaltz as well as between the Rabbi and other people. To my delight, Steve saved those tapes and promised me he would locate the box they were in. He did, and he gave me the tapes, most of which I listened to several times and transcribed. A year later, Steve called and told me he had located a second box of tapes. I went to Steve's office and was given them as well. I promptly had those tapes transcribed. God bless you, Steve.
- **Yehuda Hanegbi.** Yehuda, of blessed memory, was a gifted writer and translator who was responsible for translating and editing several of Rabbi Steinsaltz's books, including *The Thirteen Petalled Rose.* Yehuda was a special and delightful man who is deeply missed. During the years we were in contact, he gave me copies of raw translated transcripts of a number of Rabbi Steinsaltz's classes. Some of these transcripts, in edited form, made their way into a few of Rabbi Steinsaltz's published books.
- **Yehudit Shabta.** For many years, Yehudit worked with Rabbi Steinsaltz as his personal secretary, assistant, translator, and general supporter. A few times over the years, Yehudit, having great compassion for my thirst for Rabbi Steinsaltz's teachings, has sent me unpublished essays as well as essays published in obscure, now out-of-print publications.

• **Journalist interviews.** A number of times, I have had the responsibility of escorting Rabbi Steinsaltz to be interviewed by a journalist or group of journalists. During the period when the first volumes of the English translation of the Steinsaltz Talmud were published, Rabbi Steinsaltz was particularly busy with journalists from all over, including *People* magazine, the *Washington Post,* National Public Radio, and *Good Morning, America,* to name a few. I took my own notes during those interviews, knowing from personal experience that a journalist can speak to you for an hour but the resulting article usually captures a mere fraction of what was said.

• **The cutting room floor.** In 1989, the filmmaker David Rosenberg produced and directed a documentary about Rabbi Steinsaltz called *The Talmud and the Scholar,* a fifty-eight-minute video giving us a behind-the-scenes look at Rabbi Steinsaltz and his work. I am grateful to have several hours of the material left out of the video, generously given to me by David.

• **Special events.** In September 1993, Rabbi Steinsaltz and I conducted a program for several hundred Jewish educators from Hadassah International. The entire day was recorded, and I transcribed it. I also have several other videos and audiotapes of lectures that I attended. These, too, became part of the collection of sources from which I gathered pebbles.

• **Meyer Weitz.** Over the years, my friend and cousin, Meyer Weitz, attended a number of gatherings in Israel that were organized by Rabbi Emanuel Quint. Rabbi Quint wrote an important series of books titled *A Restatement of Rabbinic Civil Law,* which explains, in layman's language, the civil law of the *Shulkhan Arukh*, the Code of Jewish Law. Rabbi Quint and Rabbi Steinsaltz met during Passover and Sukkot over several years and offered public lectures. Meyer Weitz recorded these programs and sent me the tapes.

• **Newspaper and magazine articles.** I may have the best collection of clippings about Rabbi Steinsaltz in the United States. Many of these articles include interviews with the Rabbi. In addition, I've written a number of articles about Rabbi Steinsaltz over the years, based on my own interviews and conversations.

• ***Simple Words***. Rabbi Steinsaltz's book *Simple Words: Thinking About What Really Matters in Life* was based on a series of lectures the Rabbi gave to a small group in various apartments in New York City over a number of years. I attended all of those lectures, recorded some of them, and took notes. Much of the material, especially the question-and-answer periods, never made it into the book. But this omitted material supplied me with some great pebbles.

This collection of pebbles is not the "quintessential Rabbi Steinsaltz." As a serious student of illusions, optical and otherwise, I know that we can easily be blind to something right in front of our eyes. These pebbles are my selections; they are only what I have picked up. I have no doubt that along the trail, I missed a great many extraordinary pebbles that I wasn't prepared for or able to see.

As I finish this collection of pebbles, I want to offer one more that is particularly on my mind. In an introductory essay on the *Tanya,* Rabbi Steinsaltz writes:

> The earliest Hasidic masters were very sensitive about the need to keep the essential message pure by transmitting it directly from soul to soul. There is an emphasis in Hasidism on direct communications with one's Rebbe or teacher. It was felt that writing only creates a barrier.

> There was something dead about a book, and quite different from the direct communication between master and disciple, or between a teacher and pupil. There was an assumption that not only are the true problems of the soul left unresolved with books, but that the very essence of the message is somehow lost.

Rabbi Steinsaltz then tells a story about the founder of Hasidism, the Baal Shem Tov:

> During his lifetime, when a volume of sayings of the Baal Shem Tov, the founder of the Hasidic movement, came out, he dreamed that he saw a devil walking around with a book under his arm. When the Baal Shem Tov asked him what it was, the devil replied, with a smile of satisfaction, "It is a book by you, yourself."
>
> The next day, the Baal Shem Tov called his disciples together and demanded to know who dared to write books in his name. When he was shown the volume of his sayings, he read it and said, "There isn't a single word here that I actually spoke."

"The individual who makes inner contact with a holy person, showing him love and devotion, thereby supports the flow of Divine plenty in the world."

—*The Thirteen Petalled Rose*

"[David] took his staff in his hand, he chose five smooth pebbles from the wadi, and placed them in the shepherd's pouch he had in his pack. Then, with his sling in his hand, he approached the Philistine."

—*I Samuel 17:40*

Pebbles
of
WISDOM

PART I

God

"The faith of Israel is primarily a belief in the one God, who is more sublime than anything that has form or that can be conceived."

CHAPTER 1

Contemplating God

"One of the most important ways of experiencing the love and awe of God is through meditation on the Divine."

The decision to follow God

The essence of the Exodus is in the initial, faith-motivated decision to leave the ordinary, the routine life, and to follow God.

This is the all-inclusive point of departure.

Prior to that, there is nothing.

All the rest is elaboration.

Constantly standing before Him

I am here, and God is here.

What am I to do, especially since He knows not only my innermost thoughts but also how I will act them out?

Whether one meditates on this or not, for a Jew, seeing himself in this way, standing before God, is the subject for constant reflection.

There can be no uniform technique or rigid form to this contemplation, just as there is no single channel in which thought can be made to flow.

What we can say, however, is that on the one hand, it is a striving to deepen the thought, entering further into it and penetrating it with the whole of one's being.

On the other hand, it is also an effort to expand the thought, repeating it and seeking additional sides to it, finding new aspects to its possible manifestation.

One may call it a kind of creative meditation, in contrast to the mainly passive meditation practices in certain Eastern traditions.

Awareness of the Divine presence

Upon undertaking the performance of a *mitzvah*—even a very ordinary, routine action, like prayer—a person is advised to take time to prepare himself by reflecting on God, by being aware of the awe and trembling of his being before the Divine presence.

As he draws the prayer shawl over his shoulders or dons the *tefillin*, he should also be conscious of drawing the Divine light over himself.

Meditating on the Divine

It is axiomatic that one of the most important ways of experiencing the love and awe of God is through meditation on the Divine.

But not everyone has the capacity for abstract conceptualization.

A certain amount of knowledge and learning is needed.

It is difficult to meditate on the greatness of God without a minimal grasp of the laws of nature and the immensity of the cosmos.

An emotional maturity is needed in order to integrate the understanding into one's being, to convert the meditation from an intellectual truth to a power for living.

Contemplating God's greatness

If any person, wise or ignorant, great or small, will concentrate on the thought that God really fills all that exists in Heaven and earth with His glory and God sees the inwardness of man, his liver and heart, his thoughts and actions, then a kind of awareness of oneself is built up.

If a person reflects on this each day of his life, deliberately taking an hour to do so, it will become engraved in his being and have a permanent effect.

This amounts to a process of self-education, although it consists of no more than regular contemplation on the greatness and glory of God.

The time spent in such concentrated meditation is also cumulative in power, and whatever is gained becomes a firm basis for further insight.

It is often sufficient just to recollect an experience in order to reawaken its spiritual significance for oneself.

Awareness requires inner growth

The King brings one into His chamber, but one may fail to comprehend what is happening.

Only he who has reached a certain level of understanding will appreciate it.

As one of the many allegories puts it, a king went out into the fields, and a certain farmer, not knowing who the king was, offended him. The courtiers wanted to have the farmer executed on the spot, but the king said that such punishment was not equal to the crime.

Instead, he suggested bringing the man to the royal palace and educating him until he became aware of the enormity of what he had done.

In order to appreciate what God has given one, there has to be a certain level of awareness of the world and one's place in it, of Divine transcendence and human creatureliness. To awaken this awareness requires a process of education and inner growth.

Focusing and clinging to God

The demand for *kavvanah,* for focusing and clinging to God, pertains not only to prayer but also to the Grace After Meals and to every blessing that a person recites in the course of the day.

Reciting a brief blessing with *kavvanah* is even more difficult than praying with *kavvanah.*

Blessings are said often and in a variety of settings and often when neither place nor time is conducive to full concentration.

God is not an abstraction but an actuality

When asked, "What did Hasidim bring into the world?" the Kabbalistic answer, given by Rabbi Tzvi Hirsch of Ziditzov, was the following:

Let us imagine someone returning from a long journey to a distant land and telling us that he saw a bird with a human face and the legs of a horse.

Afterward, someone else goes to the land and, upon returning, says that indeed he saw the creature. But it didn't have the face of a human, although there was a certain resemblance.

And the legs were, in the abstract, like those of a horse, even if not at all identical.

Hearing this, there were more people prepared to believe the story. But there still remained many skeptics.

Whereupon a third person made the same journey and brought the very bird back with him.

This, of course, was decisive.

So, too, there are three levels of insight into the mystery of God.

First, there was a level exemplified by Rabbi Shimon bar Yochai, who came and told us about the Divine presence in the *Zohar,* which is full of such fantastic tales, strange configurations, images, and countenances that one could hardly believe him.

Then, after a number of generations, came the level exemplified by Rabbi Isaac Luria. His pupils wrote down the evidence he conveyed with all its greater attention to detail.

Finally, the Baal Shem Tov came. He exemplified the third level, and so he brought to us the very reality of the Holy One, blessed be He.

CHAPTER 2

The Inconceivable God

"God is that which cannot be grasped, and any claim to have done so can only be mistaken."

God is that which cannot be grasped

That which I can possibly understand is not the Divine.

We have here a negative sort of definition.

This is a warning to a category of persons who are self-deluded by their commonsense logic into believing that they have achieved a certain grasp of what God is.

God is that which cannot be grasped, and any claim to have done so can only be mistaken. It is like saying that one has grasped the horizon.

There are the biblical accounts of Moses and Isaiah or any of the prophets, but that is a matter of another kind of vision. Moreover, what Moses saw may have made him the humblest of men, but he was quite explicit in saying that man cannot see God and live.

The Divine essence fills everything

The Divine essence fills everything.

It is our mind that creates the barriers and forms separate existences.

Prophets, like Moses, have simply broken down these fences and separations. At Mount Sinai, the children of Israel could not endure this closeness to the Divine, and "their souls took flight," so that a sanctuary had to be built to preserve them.

The great problem of the chariot and of someone like Moses—heavy of speech and tongue-tied—is that Moses found it extremely difficult to be a man among men.

In the *Zohar,* there is a description of such persons, declaring that they are like fish of the sea walking on land.

Perhaps the world of men is like the dry land, and the Divine essence is like the vast sea surrounding the land on all sides and occasionally flooding it.

There is nothing other than God

It is said that God is One in the sense that there is nothing besides Him, both before and after the Creation.

The universe does not make any difference as far as God is concerned. He remains forever the same without ever changing. Even though we may be conscious of a world apparently apart from God, this is only the ongoing act of Creation.

The words that made the world are constantly being spoken anew, and nothing can exist unless it is sustained by them.

If they were to cease being spoken, all would revert to emptiness and chaos.

There is no before or after in God

It has been taught that the great *tzaddikim* in Heaven do not pray for the community. They can no longer relate seriously to the frivolous requests of men.

God, however, who is infinite, makes no such distinction. He hears all men equally.

There is no before or after in God, no distinction of time or place, size or value.

This means that causality, as men know it, does not necessarily correspond to the true process and cycles of existence.

To God, there is no large or small

For many clever men, the difficulty that is an obstacle to understanding God comes not from His greatness but from a basic misunderstanding of His greatness.

The person who thinks that God is justifiably concerned with the vast affairs of the galaxy and is not concerned so much about my reciting a blessing before eating a chocolate bar does not really see the greatness of God.

To the Divine Omniscience, there is no large or small, significant or insignificant detail in the infinity of the universe.

There is no difference between worlds as far as God is concerned.

How can one speak about the unspeakable?

Many books have been written about holiness and about the sense of holiness, and they all face one fundamental dilemma: How can one speak about the unspeakable?

This is the quandary of mystics, sometimes of philosophers, and even of artists.

One definition that carries with it a large measure of truth is that holiness is that which is found beyond all boundaries, that which reaches absolute infinity and absolute transcendence.

And actually, our perception of holiness can be expressed by the term—used but not coined by Freud—an "oceanic feeling," which attempts to explain or touch upon the comprehension of holiness.

A person facing the ocean for the first time, or at any other moment of heightened sensitivity, faces something grand and immeasurable, something infinite.

The feeling of "me against infinity" is, I would imagine, the basic sensation of one who stands against the holiness.

This definition is imperfect; the "oceanic feeling," like the ocean itself, is finite.

Although it is very big, it is still limited. Our perception of infinity is in many ways an attempt to grasp the unlimited, the unperceivable, that which cannot be understood, that which is, in essence, the unattainable, by its very definition.

The attempt to enter the realm of holiness is paradoxical.

Because I have entered it, then, by definition, it is not truly holy; and if it is truly holy, I shall always stand outside of it.

The reply in the Torah to Moses' prayer, his request to see the face of God, is, "You cannot see My face, for no man shall see Me and live . . . and you shall see My back parts, but My face shall not be seen" (Exodus 33:20–23).

This is the point: it is impossible to see the face. At most, we can reach an indirect, "lateral" recognition of these things, but never a direct fundamental view.

There are no words to describe the Transcendent

To illustrate the concept of a lack of words, let us take a fact from the world of physics.

Light waves have different lengths, and the ultraviolet light waves, for instance, are known to be invisible to us.

There are certain creatures, such as bees, however, that can see at least some of those ultraviolet light waves. In short, part of that which, for us, is total darkness is, for them, light.

Now the question is, what kind of light or darkness is it? We are in a situation where we have no words, or even concepts, to describe something, a color, that obviously exists.

In like manner, we can say that there are no words to describe the Transcendent.

But since, as we believe, God does wish to have some contact with us, He is prepared to suffer the imprecision of our language.

There is the little story, within another context perhaps but aptly descriptive, of one of the *tzaddikim* who suddenly stopped his prayers at a point where there was no pause.

When asked why he did so, he answered with a parable.

Once a king passed and saw a beggar playing a fiddle, and the tune pleased him so much that he stopped and invited the beggar to the palace to play before him.

Now this beggar had an old fiddle with strings that broke easily, and people told him that it was not respectful to the king to play on it before him and that it would be better to make alterations and at least fix the strings.

To which the beggar answered, "If the king wants a tune on a fine instrument, he does not lack better musicians than I. If he asked me to play before him, he took into consideration the poor state of my fiddle as well as my own limitations."

If God wishes to hear our prayers and our sincere speech with Him, He suffers our anthropomorphisms, that is, our calling on Him by names that are human and in terms that are limited in their expressiveness.

We say, "If you want us, take us as we are with all our faults and inadequacies. It is the best we have to offer."

The only thing we can do beyond that is to know that certain things are not exact or true and to be grateful for the privilege, and the audacity, to say them.

The infinite light of God has no limit

Any serious reflection on the greatness of God and His boundless mercy will lead to the realization that there is no end and no purpose to His light.

This light also remains unchanged and constant in its emanation from the Divine, and it never imposes a limit in any of its manifestations.

In contrast to the numerical, or any other, infinity, with its severe limitations in all directions but one, the infinite light of God has no limit in any direction or form.

Nothing can occur without God

On one hand, we feel God to be very near.

On the other, He is very distant.

We call Him Father.

We also call Him "*Ein Sof*—Infinite."

As the *tzaddik* said, lifting up a handful of sand and letting it run out through his fingers, "He who does not believe that every one of these particles returns exactly to the place that God wishes is a heretic."

Another image, attributed to the Baal Shem Tov, says that sometimes a great storm comes, hurls everything about, and causes the trees to shake violently so that the leaves fall.

One such leaf may drop close to a worm, and it was for this the whole world was in a furor, that a worm may eat of a certain leaf.

This, then, is the aspect of personal Providence. God's word activates and changes the world all the time. At every moment, there is a totally new state of affairs.

Whether a microbe or a galaxy, all are equally part of this and are in the same proportion to Him.

This means that God is close to us without ceasing. Nothing can occur without Him.

To be sure, it includes the bad as well as the good. For we need the flow of life in us even when we transgress.

Words like "I" and "mine" become meaningless

In certain texts, there is an extensive description of the problem of the highest level of the ungodly, of blasphemy, which is the fiftieth gate of uncleanness and is known as "Pharaoh" because Pharaoh said, "Mine is the Nile, and I made myself."

That is to say, "The river is mine. I made it, just as I made myself. I am the beginning and the end of all existence."

This is often viewed as the utmost blasphemy. When a person becomes a vehicle (or chariot) of the Divine Will, not only the concept of "I made myself" but all words such as "I" and "mine" become meaningless.

There is a custom, mostly among yeshiva students, that instead of writing, "This book belongs to so-and-so," they write, "The earth is the Lord's and the fullness thereof, and this book has been commended to the care of so-and-so."

To exist beyond the apparent limits of reality

The concept of human forgiveness is derived from the basic unconscious supposition of an omniscient presence, one that rules over time itself.

It implies a relationship between man and the absolute, a relation to God, who is beyond space and time and natural law.

Every request for forgiveness of past action on the part of man is a plea to awaken in him the "spark of holiness," the "Divine part from above," which enables him to exist beyond the apparent limits of reality.

A God I can put into my pocket is not worth being with

There was once a great *rebbe* who was asked lots of basic theological questions.

Why does God do this and that?

He answered by saying that a God that every rotten man can understand is not a God I would believe in.

If I want a God that I can put into my little pocket, it is possibly not worth being with.

If I want God to be my measure, to be exactly made to my measure and to feelings that change with every newspaper article, it is possibly not worth having such a God.

CHAPTER 3

Looking for God

"When one becomes sure that God is, that He exists, here and now, then the terror and the uncertainty are dissipated, and one can join in the adventure, or the play, of finding Him behind the partition."

God hides Himself

There is a Hasidic chant, "Thou art a hidden God."

In contrast to what one would expect, it is a joyful song.

As the Baal Shem Tov said, the Divine hiddenness ceases to be significant as soon as one knows that it is a matter of His hiding Himself and not that He isn't there.

As long as I am not sure of His existence, I am in a state of darkness.

As soon as I am convinced that he does exist, that He is merely concealing Himself, I have every reason for joy.

The hiding of the Divine countenance is terrible only because it makes it so difficult to see God—and that is the whole tragedy of the concealment.

Confronting a paradox

We are confronted with a paradox:

The contraction of God reaches such a point that the Divine countenance is hidden. Man no longer perceives God, the very source and meaning of his being.

As it has been said, the incredible greatness of the Creator lies not in the immense worlds He made but in the fact that among His creations are men who can repudiate His existence in a way that is the most extraordinary formation of all—creatures who can deny the Creator.

God hides, and we look for Him

In order for the world to exist as a coherent entity, one has to have a philosophical awareness of the fact that there is both a universe and a Creator of the universe.

In order to function, realistically, one has to assume a world that is not God, for if everything is the One God, there is no human and no other reality.

God has to descend to us and to talk in words that are comprehensible to us in order to avoid being too far away.

It is like the children's game of hide-and-seek: God pretends to hide, and we look for Him.

And then we think that He looks for us. And all the while, it is a game the Divine Omniscience plays with us for our sake.

This may be likened to the caterpillar and the cocoon it spins. Both the insect and that which wraps it up are the same.

Manifest nature, law, God's concealment, and God's essence are one. Just as the riddle is a mystery only to the one who is questioned, and the one who asks knows both the answer and the riddle.

In other words, concealment can be part of an essential unity in the dynamics of speech.

The speaker knows what is being spoken, and the one on the other side of speech, the listener, tries to penetrate the "mystery" and to understand.

God conceals Himself so that man shall seek and find Him

Two things may be said to happen when faith is a personal experience.

There is the joyful factor of the one who feels the wondrous nearness of God.

And there is the triumphal joy of God in the extrication of a person from his darkness and ignorance.

The wholly human concept of God's remoteness and inaccessibility is really another aspect of God's desire for man to come to Him.

God puts a distance between Himself and man only in order to have man cross it.

He conceals Himself so that man shall seek and find Him. Whenever man succeeds in crossing the apparent gap between them, there is a creative joy on the part of both God and man.

In man, the joy corresponds to the degree of his aspiration to bridge the gap.

In God, it corresponds to the expectation that formed a barrier intended to be burst.

Just as when a clever son is questioned by his proud father to ascertain the extent of the child's learning, he may answer one problem after another.

But the joy of the father and of the child is greatest when the test is truly difficult.

God hides, but few seek

There is the anecdote of a famous rabbi's grandson who, while playing hide-and-seek with the other children, hid himself.

The others forgot about him somehow, and after some time, the little boy ran weeping to the rabbi.

"Grandfather," he cried, "I hid myself and no one looked for me!"

Whereupon the rabbi was deeply moved and answered, "Why, that is the very same thing that God is saying all the time."

Our perception of God is limited by physical existence

A story from the Midrash tells that when God wanted to reveal His face to Moses at the burning bush, Moses was not ready and did not want it.

Then when Moses matured and asked for it, God did not want to reveal His face.

So it is for many people. One is afraid to look and thus hides his face before God. Then when he is able to see, it turns out that God has turned away.

Therefore, it is written that were the soul liberated from the body and from the senses, the capacity to realize God from the abstract knowledge we have of Him would perhaps be possible.

The very structure of our existence, however, thinking as we do through our physical brains and limited bodies, emphasizes the truth of the statement:

"And no man shall see Me and live." The other side of reality is barred.

The development of the world requires darkness

It may be said that for God to develop the photographic film of the world, He had to create a darkroom. And one needs a limited source of light, controlled and restricted, in order to function.

Once the desired effect is achieved, the windows can be opened.

The development of the world requires darkness, the hiddenness of space, and the obscuration of God Himself.

Divine revelation would most likely consume all of existence.

Reality as we know it would cease to be.

It is written that the prophet can hear the song of the celestial beings but he cannot see anything. As it was said to Moses, "For no man shall look upon Me and live."

There is this limit beyond which all is made meaningless, burned out, and extinguished.

As it is hinted in several sources in the scriptural text, any trespass of the permitted range of sanctity is a matter of utmost peril.

An expression of God's infinite power

A greater mystery than reality is the concealment of reality.

As has been said, the glory of God is perhaps the fact that among the rest of Creation there can also be an unbeliever who denies God, even though he lives by the mercy of God and reveals God with every breath of his nostrils or twitch of his finger.

That such a creature should have the capacity to deny the existence of God is an expression of God's infinite power.

Only God can cross the abyss

Sensitivity to holiness may be seen as a human capacity or talent, greater in some than in others. Holiness is not merely that which inspires. It is that which relates to God, and it is only that.

One cannot create this of oneself, even for the sake of God or in His name.

The very highest values or preferences or loves are still not holy unless they relate directly to the Divine.

One's finest creations, even if one considers them a total sacrifice to the Lord and the best humanity is capable of producing, is still far from being holy.

The gap between the human and the Divine is absolute and is not so easily bridged, either by the noblest intentions or by the most magnificent efforts. There is no way of overcoming it.

It is with this that the snake tempted Eve when it suggested that the apple could make one "like God, knowing good and evil."

It is the chief temptation of all original artists, thinkers, and men of science: the thought that by getting beyond some stage or limitation, one could be like God. The only thing that the fruit of the Tree of Knowledge seems to bring is the heartache of being more aware of God and of not being closer to God.

The Divine Himself, or the actual contact with the Absolute, remains out of reach.

It is only when God Himself reaches out to men as Revelation that there is contact; any significant approach to Him is possible only with the means made available by God.

It is He who determines the substance, and the manner of revealing the substance, of what is holy.

Only the Infinite can cross the abyss between man and Divinity.

God continuously sustains the world

The question is asked: What is the difference between human creativity and Divine Creation?

Human creativity, it is explained, is the manufacture of implements that have their own existence. They can continue to exist independently of the one who made them.

The Divine Creation, however, is continuous.

God keeps sustaining and developing what He makes by re-creating every particle of existence in endless succession.

The adventure of finding God behind the partition

Faith is not the belief that God is to be found somewhere or other.

If God is here or there, in the past or in some distant holy place, His oneness becomes rather irrelevant.

It doesn't really matter so much whether He is one or two or three or more.

The true unity of the Divine lies in the fact that there is nothing else. There is no other force or reality or significance besides Him.

When a person tries to clarify this for himself, it becomes a victory of the positive reality of the world over the otherwise confusing hiddenness of the world behind the veil. It is also a victory for God.

God rejoices in one's success in overcoming the barrier to come to Him. When one becomes sure that God is, that He exists, here and now, then the terror and the uncertainty are dissipated, and one can join in the adventure, or the play, of finding Him behind the partition.

Even the certainty that He exists is already a triumph of the highest order.

CHAPTER 4

Knowing God

"Revelation is the sudden recognition of a reality that was overlooked, because it was considered background."

Removing the sensory images that prevent one from seeing

There are two aspects of serving God.

The first is to do His will. The second is to make oneself able to see the Divine as fully as one is able to see with one's eyes.

A person achieves this by overcoming the images created by the complex of the body and animal soul's sensory organs. He must conquer and cast down the animal soul, breaking down and removing the sensory images that prevent him from seeing the Divine light.

When a person successfully overcomes this structure of falsehood, one of the world's illusions and its material nature, his Divine soul can perceive the Divine light with a vital and genuine feeling, existing and active within him at every moment of existence.

To what extent am I conscious of God's presence?

The nearness of God is not a matter of any measurable distance, just as approaching Him is not an act that is even approximately physical.

He is always where I am.

The question is whether I am here. To what extent am I conscious of God's presence?

For instance, there are a great number of things in us that the mind is not aware of. We have to learn that they exist. For example, we begin to notice the heart only if it gives us trouble, and this in spite of the fact that it is quite noisy and physiologically involved with everything we do.

There doesn't seem to be any relation between the objective reality of anything—its vital necessity or even its nearness—and the fact of our being conscious of it. On the contrary, there seems to be a curious paradox about it all.

What is close, so intimate as to be inseparable, often requires a greater amount of training and effort in order to get to know it.

God is not to be found in some other world

There are two ways of viewing the concept of "His glory filling the earth."

One can see it as children do, perhaps, as air filling all space or as something all-pervasive, like space itself.

Or else, in penetrating into the philosophical nature of the problem, we touch on a certain Kabbalistic view by which the holy letters of the Torah are not the black designations of writing but the white space surrounding them.

It is like the drawings of certain painters or the designs of Gestalt psychologists in which image and background change places depending on the viewer's emphasis.

The world can thus be seen as an image against God, who is the background, or God can become the image against the background of the world.

In either case, God is not to be found in some other world. He is somehow intrinsic to this world, constituting its very existence.

The world, possibly, manifests only the shadow of Divine existence.

Like a film projected on a screen: what we see are only the shadows cast by the light thrown against a moving series of negative pictures.

Life as a whole can justifiably be called an illusion of passing shadows, which may hold us fascinated but has no more genuineness or reality than what we give them. "Only He exists," and the world is not another reality in addition to Him. It is a shadow, or a small visible fragment of His infinity.

God is not elsewhere, in Heaven or in some invisible spiritual realm of being. He is here and everywhere, filling all with that Divine essence that is being.

In the presence of God

The Hasidic rabbi Simcha Bunim explained that every person should visualize evil as though the devil were standing over him with an ax, ready to chop off his head.

Upon hearing this, one of the disciples asked, "And what if a person cannot see himself that way?"

Rabbi Simcha replied, "That is a clear sign that the devil has already chopped off his head."

In other words, the man of God is someone who is constantly struggling. The one who does not struggle is not a servant of God.

Faith is not of itself a solution to the agony of the soul. It does not necessarily bring peace and tranquillity. On the contrary, for the great majority of men, the way of piety and scrupulous keeping of the commandments is a way of perpetual conflict and ever-increasing effort.

What does faith offer in return for the struggle and the effort?

It gives the presence of God, but not always the sense of God's presence.

A person studying the Talmud portion about the ox that gores a neighbor's cow will not necessarily achieve religious ecstasy. That is not what is promised—which is not to say that there is no relation whatever.

What is offered to the person who occupies himself with Torah and the *mitzvot* is that he will be objectively nearer to God, even if he does not feel that nearness. One has to decide what one really wants, the actual presence of God or the feeling that one is close to Him.

If one wants to feel as though one is close to God, there are many ways, from drugs to rapture induced by some technique or other. One can actually be in the presence of God, however, without having any ecstatic experience and without even knowing what is happening, that is, without any sort of great joy or enlightenment.

The bliss either comes or does not come. But no matter how one is privileged to receive a revelation, it should be viewed as a special gift.

A very clear message is always being transmitted

It is written that the voice on Sinai was a mighty voice that did not stop.

This is repeated in much of the Hasidic literature.

The voice giving the Law never stopped. It is still giving the Law, for ever and ever, for eternity.

Put another way, there is a very clear message that is always being transmitted.

The thing that has changed is that we are no longer listening.

Recognizing the obvious

The fact is that the elemental sense of the Divine is not a matter of mystical realization or any kind of emotional or cerebral experience.

It is the simplest, most fundamental perception granted to all human beings, a certainty that there is a Creator, or some sort of greater reality, responsible for the world.

It is a recognition of the obvious, not an extraordinary vision of the hidden.

A sharp consciousness of Divinity

It is said that at the revelatory confrontation on Mount Sinai, the Divine presence, the *Shekhinah,* was too much for the children of Israel. They could not bear it.

Therefore, God decided to have a sanctuary built, not only to serve Him as a dwelling but also to protect the Israelites.

Historically, this sanctuary, the Ark of the Covenant, became the geographical place, or center, from which the *Shekhinah* could emanate. But of course, this is not to be understood in the sense of a physical source of light or energy.

For the *Shekhinah* is everywhere, and there is no existence, no reality, without the *Shekhinah.*

The emanation of the *Shekhinah* should be understood rather as that which happens whenever there is a sharp consciousness of Divinity, whenever the *Shekhinah* breaks through into life and awareness.

Revelation is the recognition of a reality that was overlooked

God is present, and He dwells within everyone, just as He dwells in the world as a whole.

Except that I do not know of this Divine inner presence. As soon as I become conscious of it, however, I realize the purpose of Creation—"to be a dwelling place for Him in the world."

God creates the world in such a manner that God, being invisible, cannot be taken for granted. He has to be sought out.

There are aspects of Creation, like light, that are self-evident. Other things, including the Divine Himself, must be looked for consciously.

Like those optical illusion, inside/outside drawings, one can choose to see either the black picture against a white background or the white picture against a black background.

The play of perception depends on one's own place, one's angle or point of view.

Revelation is the sudden recognition of a reality that was overlooked, because it was considered background. It is the emergence of the essential image.

It can occur in a moment, by a slight alteration of one's perspective or will, for example, by consenting to be a dwelling place for the Divine.

God is always present

God is always present, and one can be as near to Him as one chooses. If one endeavors to approach Him by one's own efforts, it is hopelessly impossible.

In relation to the Infinite, even oral and spiritual qualities have no meaning. It does not matter whether one is Moses, the Lawgiver, or an ordinary mortal.

All stand at the same zero point before God. The great joy of the soul is savored when God comes to me, when the immeasurably great descends and fits Himself to my littleness.

And the miracle is that God remains with one always. He becomes the one reality exceeding all else.

A source of inspiration and joy to those able to grasp it

In the same way that a trained musician can read a musical score and hear the music or a mathematician can enjoy the structure and harmony of a formula, so too is the concept of Divine Unity a source of inspiration and joy to those able to grasp it.

It is a certain natural gift that has to be nurtured and developed.

The important thing is that it is a potential that exists in every man, even though, as with most gifts, there are those who are more talented and those who are less so.

Speaking with God

When a man says, "Blessed art Thou, O Lord," he finds himself standing before God, in direct confrontation with Him.

The moment a person says these words and does not wish to be a liar or a deceiver, he makes an affirmation and places himself before God.

This fact far outweighs any textual or technical consideration. In every prayer, before all else, we face this great issue. It amounts to this: when a man prays, he is addressing the Holy One, blessed be He.

I was confronted with this question not as a teacher but as a parent. Once while I was in the middle of my prayers, my little daughter tried to talk to me, and when I failed to respond, she was very angry with me, and she said, "Why don't you speak to me?"

Later on, I answered her by saying, "I was busy. I was speaking with God."

She then replied, with great understanding, that she hadn't noticed that God was answering me.

Her comment was very deep. In any event, a four- or five-year-old girl was prepared to accept the notion that I speak with God when I pray, but she wanted this to be a two-way conversation and not just a speech on my part.

Every prayer boils down, in the final analysis, to a very basic point, which are the words "Blessed art Thou," especially the "Thou." That is, I feel the presence of the "Thou" before me.

If I have someone with whom to speak, then I can pray. If I have no one with whom to speak, then what is the point of all these words and all the things I say, new, old, good, bad, ugly? What good is it if I have no feeling of presence, in the simplest sense?

CHAPTER 5

Intimacy

"God is always present, and He is closer than anything else."

Some people feel an intimacy with God

There are those who are more inclined to feel awe as a basic mode of response to the Divine and those who tend to be ashamed, remorseful, and even embarrassed by their human weakness before the Divine.

Some people feel a close relationship, even an intimacy, with God.

Like Rabbi Nachman of Bratslav, who as a boy, it is said, used to blush with shame before the Divine Omniscience every time he did or thought something he considered wrong.

The constant presence of God

The thought of Divine Unity is the core of all contemplation.

There is a story of the Hasid who, on a journey, stopped at an inn for the night. When he was asked if he desired to eat supper, he replied that he was far too tired and that all he wanted to do was go to bed at once, for he had to rise early.

He was shown to his room, and there he briskly went about making his preparations for sleep. Among other things, as was his custom, he recited the bedtime prayers, and at the right place, he concentrated on the greatness and the oneness of the Creator.

In the morning, when the innkeeper came to wake him, he found the Hasid standing, with one foot on the floor and the other on the bed, still immersed in the thought of Divine Unity.

Of course, this contemplation need not be left to the moment before retiring, and it need not be so compelling that one forgets all else. On the other hand, it is not an abstract intellectual experience.

In the endless amplitude of meaning and shades of meaning it possesses for the individual, there is something to sustain every conceivable situation and every moment in life. All that we read and study is only food for this one thought.

And when it occupies the mind, there is no room for anything else. It is the transformation of this single idea into the basis not only of a life of contemplation but also of the constant presence of God.

God is not a mental or moral entity. His nearness and support do not depend on whether one is good or deserving or whether one is correctly observing Torah and *mitzvot.*

God is always present, and He is closer than anything else.

God is closer than the beating of one's heart

Of all the pleasures in the world, the greatest is the simple joy of living.

But when does a person feel it? In rare moments—usually after emerging from a crisis—such as receiving a pardon from a death sentence or recuperating from a severe illness.

As for the presence of God—it is closer to one's being than the joy of living, closer than the beating of one's heart.

When one is conscious of it, all the rest is secondary and relatively unimportant.

God wants a living relationship

Man needs to see suffering as something given to him for his own benefit, whether as instruction or as a bitter medicine.

If it is so hidden that one fails to see it, something very serious and complicated happens to one's relationship with God—a kind of destructive bitterness.

On the other hand, the person who is ready to receive the Divine chastisement is the one who is closest to God, even though He is hidden. In chastisement, God is closer than in correct or formal relations.

As is true in ordinary human associations, rebuke is a part of genuine cherishing. The person who is prepared to accept chastisement is not simply passive and obedient.

The problem is far deeper than that. If a person is sick, he should not merely take medicine and lie in bed in order to be able to enjoy the chastisement of suffering, nor does the poor man have to resign himself to poverty.

The problem is, what is one to do with the suffering that is inflicted?

Is it in the nature of a calamity or a revelation?

The only answer lies in the certainty of interrelating with God. If there is suffering, He is contending with me, bringing me to some new appraisal of things.

He may be right or He may be wrong, in my opinion, but at least I can argue the matter with Him.

That is what God wants—a living relationship.

God reaches out to us

The contact between man and God is not a two-way but a one-way communication.

We are dependent on Him. He is not dependent on us.

He sees us. We do not see Him.

We are products of His speech, and with difficulty, we can even make out something of this speech. But any metaphor is grossly inadequate.

Let us suppose that I am talking to a young child. I understand what I am saying just as he presumably understands what I am saying. We understand each other on the level of certain words that are uttered.

Beyond that he cannot go.

But within the range of what is spoken between us, there is something of my being, a part of me, that he grasps. But only a part.

One may even say that the child is in most respects cut off from the essence of me, the speaker, and much of me is left to his imagination.

If the speaker happens to be an exceptional person, a wise man, the difference is all the greater. In that case, the speaker has had to descend even further, going to considerable lengths to make himself understood.

So, too, God may be said to have made the immeasurable descent, the enormous contraction of light and energy, in order to come into contact with us. If we do perceive something, no matter how little, it becomes the great achievement of our being.

We recognize the incalculable and unbridgeable distance between the Divine speaker and the human listener. However, when I say in prayer, "O God, cure me of my ache and trouble," it is with the irrational certainty that God had nothing better to do than to listen to my complaints, as though I were putting the fate of galaxies and my own needs on the same level.

Permitting God to enter

There is an anecdote about Rabbi Menachem Mendel of Kotzk.

He asked one of his disciples, "Where is God?"

The disciple answered, "Why, of course, He is everywhere!"

The Kotzker Rebbe shook his head and said, "Not so. He is only there where He is allowed to enter."

It may be concluded that the person who permits God to come into him is the one who is close to God. There is no need to draw and pull God to oneself or to climb and struggle to Him.

One has only to allow Him to be present. Or at least, one's actions have to be such that God can participate in them.

We are permanently connected to God

No matter who they are, whether they are those Jews with great souls who are capable of the noblest as well as the basest of deeds or people with small souls who are incapable of rising above themselves, all Jews are each and all a part of the Divine reality.

At some ultimate point in life, there is no difference between the large and small souls, the good and the bad Jews. They are all equal before God.

It is not, of course, a matter of democratic equality. The differences remain, but they are differences between brothers and sisters in the same family.

There are more successful and less successful brothers and sisters, but the fact that they are children of the same father is permanent and unchanging.

The process of creation is continuous

It is stated that God made Heaven and earth, and we say that man also makes things.

An error stems from an incorrect comparison between Divine creation and the human concept of creating or making.

In philosophical thought known as Deism, the Creator makes the world and leaves it to go by itself. Even in the Bible, there are a few instances when God seems to have abandoned the world to its own devices.

However, the whole image of a world abandoned by its Creator is based on a false analogy. The difference between human creativity and Divine creativity is not a matter of who is doing the creating but rather one of the essence of the created thing and the act of creation.

For example, let us take a living creature that has already matured and been made whole. At the same time, the body has to renew itself continuously. There has to be ever-additional creation for the body to remain alive.

This points to the difference between the completion of a design and the process of creation. The process of creation is continuous.

At the same time, it follows a pattern of growth, of individual completion and disintegration.

The world is sustained by the continuous "saying" of the same Ten Utterances forever. The work of man is actually secondary and external.

Man merely alters the shape of the original substance, whereas the Divine action is that of making something come into being where nothing at all existed.

The simple human emotion of gratitude

If someone loves me or goes out of one's way to do me good, it is difficult to avoid responding positively. It is one of the most natural things in human nature.

How much more so if the other is a great and mighty King who bends down to exalt a lowly person like myself and showers me with tenderness and affection.

Besides the automatic response of great love, there is boundless gratitude because I know how unworthy I am.

Our relationship with God should include the simple human emotion of gratitude to Him who gave us all we possess. But we are not thankful, in contrast to animals and children, for instance, who are on the whole far more inclined to show gratitude.

This stubborn distortion in the heart, this inability to respond in a simple, natural manner to Divine love and goodness, is perhaps our worst infirmity.

Awakening the natural impulse to love God

There is no essential difference between the love of God and the love of man. But since the love of God is not described in numberless publications sold at corner kiosks, with illustrations and cartoons, the matter seems to be much more difficult.

True, there is an intrinsic difficulty. Love of God depends on one's ability to be aware of Him, not in the sense of one's knowledge of what is written in this book or another, but in terms of personal consciousness.

One can love God to the degree that one is able to be conscious of Him or to feel Him.

All that is necessary is to understand and to sincerely inquire into one's knowledge of that which is worthy of love, and the natural impulse, the love of God, is awakened.

Nothing should interfere with acts of gratitude to God

In response to God's unremitting graciousness to man, His reduction of Himself to enable man to grow freely, man should abandon all else and hold fast to whatever he knows of Divine reality.

Nothing should prevent him from devoting himself to God.

Neither body nor soul, neither inner nor outer forces, should interfere with his acts of gratitude to God.

Even one's wife and children, money, and honor should be regarded as having no value in themselves, compared to that which is God.

A genuine fear of God

There is a story of the *tzaddik,* the saintly person, who, after passing through a forest, said that he was amazed at the awe and fear of God he had seen displayed by some nameless person there.

An uncouth and unlearned youth had been standing among the trees, shouting at his father, "Were I not afraid of God, I would smash your head with my ax!"

This indicated, said the *tzaddik,* that the youth had overcome a powerful urge to kill his father and had done so because of a genuine fear of God.

"Such a victory," said the *tzaddik,* "is more than I can claim for myself, never having struggled with such a terrible passion. And I am humbled by it. I am not at all sure whether I or those around me would be able to make the same sacrifice."

One fears God because one feels Him

Rabban Yochanan ben Zakkai told his pupils that he hoped they would experience fear of Heaven in the same way they experienced fear of man. That is, the experience should be vivid physically, emotionally, and intellectually.

It is not just a deep inner conviction but something that compels appropriate action.

One cannot fear God as a witness, as one who merely looks on. One fears God because one feels Him, both within oneself and without.

He is "here," and my life as a whole reacts accordingly.

CHAPTER 6

Faith

"Faith is one of the attributes of human character. Its scope and power are a function of both inheritance and cultivation."

The path of faith

The people of Israel were slaves in body, mind, and spirit. They had no spiritual content or any real goal in life. The only thing they did have was a vague sense of continuity, an obscure link with their forefathers.

This is what prevented them from assimilating completely with the Egyptians and what prepared them for what they were about to be given.

Then came the call to depart from Egypt. The very desire for freedom was a tremendous revolution in the soul of this nation of slaves. It was the awakening of the need for inner freedom that exists in the soul of every individual.

Although they did not yet know God and had no idea as to how the Exodus would in fact occur, they believed. The slaves had neither knowledge nor understanding, and yet they went out into an unknown and unmapped desert.

Such a spark of faith can enable those who possess it to overcome all dangers and obstacles.

This path of faith is almost bereft of profound intellectual content, but it creates a link that goes much deeper than that of any other kind. It is a relationship of devotion, of inner oneness beyond perception, with the Divine.

This decision, this inexplicable faith, conceals the seeds of all that will in due course be revealed. This is where the relationship begins and where its character is shaped. The overt, external revelation occurs at a later stage. But the inner, essential relationship is there from the very beginning, from the very first act of faith.

This is why the people of Israel were able to say, prior to the giving of Torah, "We shall do and we shall harken" (Exodus 24:7), because their essential link with the Torah, although hidden, was there from the first.

Getting stuck with infantile images of God

A picture of Divine glory in the minds of children can persist throughout life, with infantile images of the "grand old man in the sky" serving to obstruct mature inquiry into the nature of the Divine.

Indeed, one's level of consciousness can be said to be the decisive factor in all of one's emotional relationships.

If a person remains at the level of consciousness of a three-year-old, his emotional life will tend to remain at about the same level.

God really does exist

My late uncle once quoted the great Rabbi of Kotzk, who said, in light of the story of Judah and Tamar in the Bible, that every man must have a close friend, so close that he can reveal his heart to him and even tell him that he has had dealings with a prostitute.

Today, one can talk about such things in the street with anybody.

But today one needs a close soul-friend, to whom one can tell that one believes in God, to tell him that despite the fact of being religious and carrying out the *mitzvot,* "I nevertheless believe in God."

I think that part of the job of religious education is in the personal ability to throw off the philosophical, intellectual, and academic baggage that has become an encumbrance rather than a staff to support us and to say what many people think in their hearts: that God really does exist and that it is actually possible to turn to Him.

The power of faith

The faith of a simple Jew comes not from an intellectual understanding and fear of the Divine but from an intrinsic love of God.

This love is strong enough to nourish the life of the nation. What is more, every Jew is given such a root, or source of power, in his soul, which can be drawn on endlessly—a human energy source, so to speak.

After one has exhausted the external sources, one penetrates into the abyss of oneself and draws forth the passion and power that are hidden there. Recognizing this vast potential, one can tap it and make it serve the purposes of daily life.

But how is this to be done?

How can one use this power, which is in one and yet beyond one, which is so terrifying that one spends a lifetime trying to keep it within bounds? How can one dole it out in controllable portions and live with it?

One recommended way is that of constant self-exhortation to make the intellectual effort to maintain control over oneself and to develop consciousness. And on the other hand, there is the admission that the source of all power and effectiveness is in the unconscious depths.

Faith is given to us as an inheritance

Faith is not something we necessarily have to achieve by ourselves. It is given to us as an inheritance.

For certain people, it may be the end product of a lifetime of trial and error, thought and contemplation.

But for the Jewish people, it is also a legacy from our forefathers. The splendor of the Jewish heritage is the certainty that wherever and however one is situated, God is nearer than all else.

Faith is the key that ensures the joy of life

The recurrent question has always been, "What is the key?"

The answer that is always given is, "The righteous shall live by his faith." Faith is the key that ensures the joy of life.

The joy of life is the same as the joy of existence itself. No matter what one's destiny, whether to be a sinner or a saint, rich or poor, happy or wretched, the one great and decisive factor is joy in the knowledge that God is present.

The more sincere this conviction, the more intense and alive one feels, because everyone lives by one's faith.

Doubt is always present

Doubt strips a person of the power to act and think meaningfully by making him wonder whether a thing is true or not, by making him believe that he has no certainty about anything. Indeed, doubt is always present.

One may take even the most familiar word or fact, and by repeating it over and over, there enters an element of doubt, an uncertainty about its form and content.

Everyone is acquainted with the sudden loss of assurance about a date, a person's name, a place, or anything well known.

One becomes vexed about forgetting and wonders whether one ever knew it properly.

Most concepts of belief are acquired in the kindergarten years

Many people say, "I don't believe," and they may even be convinced of it in all sincerity. But it is not so simple.

Heresy and atheism require that a person should at least know what he is rejecting.

When the modern Jew declares, “I don’t believe,” he is really saying that he does not believe in the things that religious people believe in.

Most concepts of belief and of Jewishness are acquired in the kindergarten years, with perhaps occasional additions in the preparation for bar mitzvah. When these childish conceptions confront a man’s adult knowledge, it is no wonder that they are promptly rejected as inappropriate in the declaration “I don’t believe.”

Often enough, someone who considers himself a wicked and even sinful person is only an innocent who does not even know enough to ask the right questions.

Paradoxes, unanswered problems, and logical contradictions

One can ask all kinds of questions without those questions undermining one’s faith.

I was once a student of mathematics. I know about so many unanswered problems and so many paradoxes and so many logical contradictions in mathematics.

Do these things undermine my belief or understanding of mathematics?

Not at all.

The recognition of a Higher Power is not a matter of faith

The Holy One, blessed be He, existed before Creation, and He continues to exist, unchanged, in the hereafter and forever. This brings to mind the explanation offered by the Tzemach Tzedek to the philosophical problem of faith.

There is a *mitzvah* to believe in God, he says, but it may be defined as an injunction to believe that the "Lord is God"—that the transcendental and immanent are of the same essence.

The recognition of the reality of a Higher Power, a Creator and Omniscient Presence, is not a matter of faith. It is more a matter of a point of view. It belongs to the field of one's vision.

The Torah does not obligate one to believe in the soul. One feels it instinctively, and there is no need for specific instruction.

The way to faith is never smooth

The path to faith is not easy, neither for someone who has grown up in a "religious" home nor for one who has grown up in a secular atmosphere.

And this is not surprising. The way to faith is never smooth.

It is not for anyone a broad and even highway along which people progress at the same pace; it is always a tortuous, winding path—very personal and private.

A certain *tzaddik* put it with profound simplicity:"Because I know that God is great, because I know that I alone know and no one else can know as I do, someone else may know more than I do, know more deeply, more comprehensively, more perfectly.

"But in the end, the experience of God is personal and unique and can never be transferred to another."

The Torah does not command us to believe in God

The commandment to believe in God is not a commandment to believe in His existence, because that is something we can see on our own.

Faith is what we cannot see on our own.

The concept of "faith," more precisely understood, relates to believing something about the Divine nature, the fact that "the Lord is God"—that is to say, that the transcendental and the immanent are one.

"I am the Lord your God" (Exodus 20:2), the commandment to believe in the Divine Being, is not a commandment to believe in the existence of a Creator but rather to believe in the unique bond between the unfathomable Being beyond all existence and "the Lord your God who brought you forth from the land of Egypt"—the Omnipotent, Active Power in the world.

Awareness of the existence of God, the Supreme Power, Creator and Activator of being, is related not to faith but to vision: "From my flesh I see the Divine" (Job 19:26). We can perceive Him with a palpable consciousness in the same way that we see physical objects.

That is why the Torah does not command us to believe in the existence of God, just as it does not command us to believe in the existence of our souls and bodies, because we can sense these by ourselves.

There is a gladness in Heaven when man passes the Divine test

The most difficult question that God poses is that of His Divine existence.

We have to grapple with a whole set of barriers and errors and confusions.

But when we succeed in breaking through, we not only feel the closeness of God but also delight in God's pride in us.

There is a gladness in Heaven when man passes the trials and barriers of the Divine test.

PART II

The Seeker

"Our goal is to always aim for greater heights, to be constantly struggling and striving to do better and to be closer to God."

CHAPTER 7

The Soul

"A loose definition of the soul is the spiritual entity that gives life to a person and of which the body is its material aspect."

The ways in which the soul is clothed

It is said that the soul has three garments: thought, speech, and action. The word "garment" refers to anything that conceals and covers, as well as what is expressed or revealed to the outer world.

The garment of thought is the inner clothing revealing the soul of the person to himself.

The garment of speech is the outer expression of the soul in terms of ideas.

The garment of action is the manifestation of the soul through the instruments of the physical world.

Such are the ways in which the soul as a whole is clothed.

The soul clothes itself in the blood of man

The concept of a garment or clothing in Jewish wisdom is intended to indicate that which serves both to cover or hide as well as manifest or reveal.

It is the way in which a person is concealed and protected from the outer world and the way in which he is seen and apprehended by the world.

For example, it may also be, to get beyond physical terms, the relation between speech and thought. Thought clothes itself in speech, with speech revealing thought, serving as its vehicle of expression, and yet at the same time hiding the thought, unable to transmit it completely, and thus becoming its substitute.

It has been said that the soul clothes itself in the blood of man.

The soul may be likened to a person driving a car

In the struggle between body and soul, the question to be decided is not only who is stronger but also who will rule over the other.

At first, there is the overcoming of one over the other, the taming.

The body becomes an instrument for the soul, and the body ceases to act on its own wishes.

For example, the soul may be likened to a horseman or to a person driving a car.

Not being familiar with the way the engine works, the driver may imagine that it operates by itself, that is to say, in accordance with the laws of its own structure.

Only after a long period of using the car does the person begin to realize that it is an extension of himself.

It doesn't have a will of its own, nor is it likely to rebel against him.

Only when the body is completely controlled does the soul feel free, because so long as the soul has to clench the reins tightly and struggle against the body, it cannot feel inspired or exhilarated.

Only when the soul reaches a degree of genuine control over matter does it, as it is said, "blaze forth."

Released and pure, it can do as it pleases.

Which is what is meant by the saying that he who truly sees this world as it is in his lifetime is privileged to possess the next world.

For the difference between the next world and this world is not one of place but one of the power of the soul, the extent to which the soul can be free.

If a person reaches that stage wherein the soul rules the body as though the body doesn't exist anymore as something with a desire of its own, then his soul exists here in the same way as it would in Paradise.

The central issue in life is the victory of the soul over itself

The daily prayer book of the great Hasidic leader Rabbi Schneur Zalman of Liadi, known as the Baal haTanya, contains a rather surprising commentary that says that there are souls who have descended to earth only to suffer for seventy years, and God has no other need of them but that.

God does not need their Torah learning or their good deeds or anything else but their suffering for His sake.

This seems cruel, but its intention is really to ease the pressure, to tell us that it is not a matter of accomplishments—how many pages of Talmud have you learned or how many *mitzvot* have you performed.

The central issue of life is clearly defined as the victory of the soul over itself, the overcoming "in spite of."

After all, people are human in their weakness, and God knows what each person is.

Is it not said that God never imposes a test on a man that the man cannot successfully pass and that the greater the man, the more severe the test?

The two souls of man

It is written in the Kabbalah (*Etz Chayyim* 50:2) that there are two souls in every person, irrespective of the nature of that person: the Divine soul and the animal soul.

And the differences between people—in breadth of outlook or goodness of character—can perhaps be traced to the quality of one or another of these two souls.

The constant struggle between the two souls of man

In Genesis (25:23), a verse tells of Jacob and Esau, the twins who were already in conflict in Rebecca's womb.

The conflict was causing Rebecca such trouble that she had to ask God about it.

She was told that two personalities, two nations, were to be born out of the one seed and that each would go its separate way.

The essence of the matter is that everyone contains not two sides to one being but two separate souls.

No ordinary person can be so sure of himself that he will know exactly where he is going.

He is always open to some other force within himself that may reorient him.

There is a constant struggle between the two souls of a man, and one of the most enduring aspects of a human personality is its changeability, its tendency to flip and to be something else.

Most men strive and hope to reach some level of decency, goodness, or even holiness.

But frequently there is a sudden turn for the worse, an unexpected upheaval in which the person looks at himself with shame and horror.

The animal soul as tempter

A pure human soul that is undivided and static does not, and perhaps cannot, exist. Without anything to struggle against, without any resistance, there is no progress.

As the Hasidim used to say, "If God wanted man to be like that, He would have done better to create a few million more angels."

The angels are limited. They are static, and each is eternally the same. The human soul needs to be challenged by the animal soul for the sake of the individual's growth, and it is not fair to call the animal soul evil because it merely does its duty.

Its duty is to tempt; its deepest hope is that the person is not tempted.

In a famous story in the *Zohar,* the king hired a courtesan to lure his son into evil ways, wishing she might fail.

The dilemma of the courtesan, the animal soul, is obvious.

Five levels of the soul

In Jewish tradition, there are at least five different levels of the soul, all of them difficult to translate into other languages.

A loose definition of the soul is the spiritual entity that gives life to a person and of which the body is its material aspect.

Levels within levels in the soul

Three of the levels of soul—the vital soul, known as *Nefesh;* the spirit, known as *Ruach;* and the Divine soul, known as *Neshamah*—have within them at least three levels of the same order.

In other words, *Nefesh* is divided into the *Nefesh* of the *Nefesh,* the *Ruach* of the *Nefesh,* and the *Neshamah* of the *Nefesh.*

And this is only a partial indication of the complexities of the soul.

Which soul will rule the other?

What the Divine soul wants is that all the *sefirot,* the ten attributes of the soul, from wisdom (*Chokhmah*) to kingdom

(*Malkhut*), in thought, speech, and action, and all the forces and organs of the body, should be a vehicle of the expression of holiness.

Evidently, the animal soul and the Divine soul desire the very opposite thing, and each wants the whole of a person.

The question is, who will rule?

CHAPTER 8

Searching for One's Purpose in Life

"Just as the miner is lowered into the depth of the earth to bring up the valuable ore, so too is the Divine soul lowered into the body and its darkness, to seek out the precious stones and minerals in the animal being. This may well be the purpose of the Creation altogether."

A descent for the sake of ascension

The questions may be asked, "Why did God create a world and clothe the light of one's Divine soul in the 'skin of the serpent' and in a 'fetid drop' like the body?"

For the human body is flesh, like all animal flesh, and in addition, it has the animal soul, which is like having the human body in the serpent's skin.

The answer is that God introduced the Divine soul into the physical body in order to lift it up.

It was not a descent of punishment.

It was a descending for the sake of ascending and raising up, in order to make the elevation an achievement.

Just as the miner is lowered into the depth of the earth to bring up the valuable ore, so is the Divine soul lowered into the body and its darkness to seek out the precious stones and minerals in the animal being.

This may well be the purpose of the Creation altogether.

Spirituality is not, by definition, holy or glorious

Because we are physical beings, we are tied to matter and material things.

We presume somehow that these represent reality. The ability to get beyond the idea that reality contains things other than those that a simple monkey can feel is an opening.

In itself, it doesn't mean much.

But it means the ability to acknowledge the overwhelming value of those things that are not touchable, not seeable, and so many times don't even cost money.

It's a gateway. It is not, in itself, an answer.

Every person is spiritual. Most of our inner feeling is not connected with the material world. Love is a spiritual manifestation. Hatred is also spiritual.

Spirituality in and of itself is a different realm from the material world. It can be secular, and it can be religious. It can also be evil.

Spirituality is not, by definition, holy or glorious.

In many places where you have a shallow notion of the world, you don't have an understanding of the reality of evil.

But evil exists.

Evil has spiritual manifestations. Lots of them.

You can have a completely evil spirituality.

The importance of finding one's purpose

Every individual has a definite function within the people, just as every limb or organ has its function in the body.

One of the chief problems a person has to solve for himself is to know what his function is.

There is the story of the *tzaddik* who said to a rich but stingy disciple of his entourage, "You're in great danger."

"Why?" asked the disciple.

"Because," said the *tzaddik,* "every army is composed of many units, regiments, platoons, and so forth, and if a person takes upon himself to move from one unit to another, he is liable to be punished as a deserter. And you, who were supposed to belong to the brigade of philanthropists and givers of charity, have deserted to the brigade of Torah scholars."

In many respects, a person may be convinced of doing the right thing, but it may not be the right thing for him.

Each person has a special gift

Each person has a special gift in some particular field of endeavor. It is in that field that he is called on to make a special contribution.

The sages say that in addition to keeping all the commandments, one should choose a single observance to be particularly scrupulous and diligent about.

One can be guided in this choice by the promptings of one's own heart and inclinations.

As the masters of moral education said, one who has a talent for cutting precious stones should not be a lumberjack, for to do so would be to spurn a gift bestowed by the Creator.

The soul may repeat a lifetime

What we call ego, I, self, is a combination of body and soul.

The soul may repeat a lifetime, with a different body, until that person has fulfilled whatever this soul had to do.

The soul is an entity. It is the same soul. It returns.

I may not recognize it, but it is still the same soul.

Reincarnation is part of official Jewish theology.

In some cases, people who die are reborn entirely or almost entirely as the same psyche.

This may happen one time or many times.

We speak about a person having to achieve certain things within a span of a lifetime.

We make so many mistakes. Sometimes when we look backward, we see that things we considered important were really unimportant and that things we considered essential were really trivial.

The idea is that most people cannot complete what they are supposed to do in one lifetime because they wander in lots of directions.

It is like a pupil who is sent back to do a class again and repeat it until he gets what he has to understand.

This is our official theology, even though I'm afraid that a lot of rabbis won't say it.

The souls of two people can grow into a genuine unity

As long as a person identifies himself with his body and concentrates all his attention on a particular "I" in time and space, he can never really love another person.

He can only love himself, because the "I" is the focus of his whole being.

By way of contrast, when the soul is seen as the mainspring of one's being and as the meaning of life, there is no limit to the possibility of love because no two bodies can ever become one.

At best, they can make good use of each other.

Two souls, however, that strive together toward the primal root of things come closer and closer.

And if they continue on an ever-higher plane, they can grow into a genuine unity.

The greatest happiness is the pleasure of being alive

To feel true happiness, it is perhaps necessary to go through the darkness of pain and the pit of anguish.

In order to truly know happiness, one must make a place for it in oneself, and this can best be done by great pain, which thrusts all else aside.

For example, the greatest happiness of all, the pleasure of being alive, is hardly ever experienced in ordinary circumstances.

And only when life is threatened, in passing through the danger of death, does one know it fully.

In other words, only when a person realizes the full pain and terror of his life can he make a place for God in himself.

There is a path that leads upward

The Jewish view of world history is optimistic, but it is optimism with substance and meaning. The hope that it offers depends on us.

It can be summarized like this:

Humanity is born into the perfect world of the Garden of Eden and begins to descend into decadence and immorality.

But this downfall is only part of the story. At the same time, there is another, parallel momentum, a path that leads upward, step by step, sometimes revealed and sometimes hidden.

This inexorable process leads to redemption.

And when that process is complete, man and the entire world will ascend to their point of departure and even transcend it.

Becoming absorbed in the task of Divine work

A person should see himself as part of a caravan that is climbing a high mountain. His body and soul are on call, ready to do whatever is needed.

When one is busy with one's hands, one is doing God's actions.

When thinking or feeling, one is occupied with God's thoughts. When speaking, one is uttering His words.

Such a life is called "soul restoring" in that Torah brings the soul back to its source. As it is said, "The precepts of the Lord are right, rejoicing the heart" (Psalms 19:1).

Their capacity to make the heart rejoice came from the fact that no matter who the person is, whatever his level, when he does the will of God, he knows that he is redeeming the world and redeeming his soul.

The sanctified deed extends in unknowable ways far beyond the confines of the action.

In such a life, a person forgets the personal accounts of his own self and becomes absorbed in the task of Divine work.

The person who has not found God has not labored hard or long enough

Evidently, there are different kinds of souls.

There are those that are more sensitive and less sensitive to holiness, as well as higher and lower in some basic fashion according to their essence.

A soul that is less sensitive may have to labor more in order to reach certain levels of being that are natural to a higher soul.

As the sages have maintained, if someone says, "I have struggled and found," one should believe him.

If a person claims that he has not found God, it means that he has not labored hard or long enough.

Like buried treasure that can only be recovered by digging deep enough, his fear of Heaven is usually hidden in the depths of the heart, and considerable effort is needed to draw it forth.

Why children are often wise

One of the reasons why children are often wise is that they have so much natural humility, which is the capacity to absorb things without having to relate to them critically.

This may be considered a requirement for creativity of all kinds, artistic and scientific.

Among modern physicists, the period of youth is usually known to be the time of innovation and creativity, while the later years are devoted to elaboration and teaching of the original inspirations.

What is life? What is it all for?

The book of Ecclesiastes is a key to a more inward-directed Judaism, posing as it does the great questions: What is life? What is it all for?

These are the basic questions of every thinking person. And in the course of the book, all the substantial, rational, and usual solutions to this question are demolished, again and again.

What is the purpose of life? Certainly not any one of the possibilities that Ecclesiastes raises, telling us of his own experience and eventual despair.

The essential conclusion of the book, in terms of the answer to the fundamental question, is that there is no way of finding the purpose of life within the framework of physical life itself.

And if we pursue this line of thought, we reach a conclusion that if there is a purpose to life, it has to be beyond life.

The special key to the private door

When we pray, saying, "Give us our portion in your Torah," it is to let us have the merit and the good fortune to grasp our own private portion of the Torah.

For the Torah has so many locks and keys, and each key is individual, each doorway is one's own.

A person can be considered very fortunate if he finds the special key, the private door that is his to enter.

Too often people just keep wandering about, getting involved with other people's keys and doors.

They make mistakes and get themselves confused and entangled in points of view not their own.

The simplest solution is to be certain that one's connection to Torah exists.

If one just lets attention be properly oriented, it is possible to feel that certain sentences in prayer, certain passages of Scripture, have special appeal to oneself. They speak to one.

Many Jews will learn these passages by heart, becoming emotionally intimate with certain words that serve for them as a doorway.

Some people find this key to the realm of intellectual content.

Others, in the doing of certain actions, the performance of *mitzvot,* and this has as much meaning for them as the complex idea of the intellectual or mystical experiences of the Kabbalist.

All lead to the inner chambers of the Divine presence.

The point is that for each seeker, such a key is the hidden secret of one's destiny.

Beyond rational explanation, it remains beautiful and personally meaningful for a significant period of time, if not for all of one's life.

The other side of the same truth is that each one is expressing the same thing, the same melody, in six hundred thousand voices.

For every person has his own unique voice, even when the song is the same.

CHAPTER 9

Spiritual Progress

"When a person feels that things are going smoothly, when he feels that there are no obstacles on his road to holiness—this is a clear sign that he is lost."

The spiritual life has become dominated by a shallow standard of measure

We are living in an age of psychological values. Everything is measured by the effect on one's subjective thoughts and feelings.

Does it inspire one? Does it depress one?

And the spiritual life has also become dominated by the same shallow standard of measure.

It is very like the confusion in estimating simple things like eating. One may or may not enjoy one's food. It has nothing to do with the need to eat in order to live.

All calculations of who is a saint and who is a sinner belong to God

It is forbidden for me to judge my fellow man. It is not for me to decide whether he is innocent or guilty.

That may sometimes be the task of a court. But as it is written in Jewish law, once a person has received his punishment, he is again a pure soul, as far as I or any other man of Israel is concerned.

All these calculations—who is a saint and who is a sinner—all belong to God. Only He can make them.

As the Rambam (Maimonides) said, a person who is bad is inscribed for death, and if we observe that all sorts of people go merrily on their way, it is because we don't know how to make the reckoning.

We may calculate according to our reason, but God makes His reckoning according to the truth of the Divine attributes.

In other words, we cannot possibly ever make any final judgments about anyone.

In keeping with the *mitzvah* to hate the evildoer who has been rebuked and yet persists in his sinfulness, it is not a judgment passed against him, damning him to Hell and purgatory. It is part of the need to hate and to love at the same time.

The ability to see depends on one's purity of heart

In the Holy Land, a person has to be in a condition of readiness in order to see its light.

A person may come to the Holy Land from the Diaspora and bring with him all the shells of those other lands.

He may be so wrapped up in them that he cannot see anything.

The ability to see depends on one's purity of heart, and the ability to distinguish one place from another requires a certain readiness for change.

Moving a dying man from a place of sadness to a place of merriment won't make much of a difference. He will still feel the gloom of his approaching end.

Our vision is limited to a narrow range

The reality of the world is nowadays apprehended in terms of electromagnetic fields.

But when I look at the world, I do not see electromagnetic fields, nor do I perceive any diagrammatic representation of a mathematical formula.

What I see is table, chair, arm, and leg—which is to say that my organs of perception do not see.

It is known that our vision is limited to a narrow range of light waves of a certain size. From this we may conclude that we have to use our understanding to see that which our vision cannot ascertain.

In the same way, since the eyes of the body cannot hope ever to see the Holy One, blessed be He, the problem is one of using the right means of explanation.

The aspiration to perfect the soul and elevate the world

From the human point of view, life is life, the main goal of life being life itself. Religious Jewish life, however, is not "just life." It contains certain goals and missions.

According to this view, living well means fulfilling life's mission.

This mission contains many parts and details, yet its essence is to perfect the body, the soul, and the world, in the framework of an ongoing relationship with God.

This mission is to be fulfilled not at a certain age or life period but rather in each and every part of life and in any situation in which one finds oneself.

The system of commandments, in its entirety, shows that there is nothing, either in time or in place, that does not somehow pertain to worshiping the Almighty and to the aspiration to perfect the soul and elevate the world.

Every nook and cranny in the Jew's life is surrounded by commandments, and the Jew is obligated to fulfill them at each and every moment.

So long as he does so properly, he fulfills life's aim.

True, everything has its own proper time and age. Yet in no time and age is one exempt from God's worship.

In every age, one has different roles, according to his strength and ability at that specific age and situation; and just as there are special functions for the young adult, so there are other roles that one is bound to fulfill as one progresses along the course of life.

According to Judaism, the course of life, of real life, is not seen as an ascent toward adulthood and from then on only descent.

Rather, it is an uninterrupted journey "from strength to strength."

Starting out life as an amorphous, inchoate mass, a utensil that has not yet taken shape, man goes on to acquire a more complete form, which he keeps shaping constantly through much study and good deeds, along with a constant perfection of body and soul, by directing them toward the real aim of life.

Seeing life as a whole, all of whose parts are equally important, gives a very different evaluation of life.

Once man builds this ability to live in the present, to live life as it is, without picturing imaginary ideals, he can live old age just as happily as the young adult, in the peak of his vigor.

For the inevitable physical changes of old age are usually accompanied by parallel spiritual changes, which give man the possibility not to feel these physical changes, emotionally, at all.

When one puts aside all those imaginary aspirations that cannot be fulfilled, one can draw and enjoy goodness from every point along the path of life and live life itself.

The same place can be holy to one person and commonplace to another

It is maintained that in Israel, there is a greater concentration of holiness.

If, as not infrequently happens, a person complains that he is not aware of any more holiness in Israel than elsewhere, the answer is that he himself is to blame, not the Holy Land, and that he should work on himself and repent and try to make himself a more effective receptacle of spirit.

The perception of holiness belongs to the perceiver as well as to that which is perceived.

Just as the same book can be profoundly meaningful to one reader and utterly meaningless to another, the same place can be holy to one person and commonplace to another.

The festivals are internal events in the life of the individual

Whenever we remember a historical event, we connect ourselves not so much with the facts as with their psychological and emotional significance.

If we want to understand the personal, inner meaning of a festival, we should look to its intrinsic spiritual essence.

We should see the festivals as internal events in the life of the individual, which are reflections of the collective life of the nation.

This approach will open a door for us toward a wider, albeit not immediately apparent, understanding.

One should compare people on the basis of their efforts

It is not possible objectively to compare men in terms of their transgressions, because this is not the correct gauge of worth. One should compare them on the basis of the degree of effort required to overcome temptation.

What for one person is a terrible temptation, on account of his personality or history, is for another of no import whatsoever.

For a gambler, playing cards has a different weight than for someone who has never played.

It is always easier to tell someone else to overcome a wrong impulse. The question is whether I myself can do as much even if I am a very righteous person.

It is not necessarily a matter of correcting conspicuously appalling sin but rather of the ordinary virtuous man's capacity to flee from the passionate urges of his own heart, to avoid the evils of slander and other such seemingly trivial modes of behavior like thoughtless speech or careless dealing in money transactions.

What a child learns has to be correct

One should not educate the child to believe something that is correct only for one's childhood and has to be changed for more correct beliefs later on.

"He'll understand when he grows up."

On the contrary, the child has to be helped to understand in accordance with his capacities, but what he learns has to be correct, so that even when he grows up, he won't find any discrepancies—it will still be correct.

The capacity for self-deception is enormous

There is a story about a hermit scholar who devoted himself entirely to Torah and prayer in a little room that he never left.

Once he thought he detected the sounds of an audience, of people quietly gathered on the other side of the closed door to listen to his devotions.

He tried to pay no attention to this rustling noise, but he did experience a heightened fervor at the thought that he could awaken others to devotion, and he prayed more vehemently than ever.

He continued for months and years until he felt himself on such a high plane of spiritual achievement that he could now show himself.

He opened the door and found that the rustling noises he had been hearing were made by a family of cats who were living there. For years, he had been praying for one litter of kittens after another.

The capacity for self-deception is enormous.

Moving but staying in the same place

I had a friend. He was older than me, but for a time I became his teacher. He was on a long path to religion, and it was for him a way of suffering.

At one point, I told him about "procession caterpillars." They go in a line, one after the other. You see a whole line of caterpillars, each touching the other, and they are going in a procession.

Perhaps they are searching for food. Biologists experimented with them, and one experiment had almost political implications.

One caterpillar leads. The others follow.

Why is the leader a leader? What made him into being a leader?

And they found out that the leader is a leader because each has the instinctive feeling to follow the tail of another caterpillar.

Now, there was one caterpillar who didn't find a tail, so he became the leader. By default.

So that's the leader—the one that didn't find a tail.

In order to prove it, they did something that is in a way unkind. They arranged them to form a circle, the first caterpillar touching the last.

They work by instinct, and so they walk in a circle. And they go like this until they die. Always in the same circle.

I said to my friend that sometimes people go in this kind of circle in their spiritual life, and the only way to solve it is to cut it.

You have to cut the caterpillar-like circle by will, and then you may go in any direction.

The circle means death, moving but staying in the same place.

There are people who lead that sort of life for years, and I'm not speaking just about material ways of life but spiritual as well.

A person has all kinds of driving impulses but no solution.

You come to the same questions, the same answers, and so you move in a circle.

You don't move anywhere.

What will I get out of the next life?

A great number of civilized human beings live comfortably with the notion that they would like to know God.

This is as much of a search for meaning as they can indulge in.

They do not get beyond the daily obligations of ethics and religion. Their search is, at best, the search for an earthly fortune, a matter of putting effort into something and getting a more or less just compensation.

There is the story of the rich man who asked the rabbi, "What will I get out of the next life?"

The rabbi answered, "At least as much as you invest in it."

If you put a lot of money and effort into an earthly endeavor, you are likely to earn even more. If you put a lot of thought and energy into your spiritual endeavors, you're liable to gain more in the Heavenly hereafter.

The trouble is that too many people are much more troubled about the loss of a twenty-dollar bill on earth than about losing a spiritual opportunity to perform a kindness.

CHAPTER 10

Repentance

"We believe that the main duty, the chief work, of man is to make corrections."

Repentance is a total upheaval

There are actually two levels of repentance.

One level of repentance is when a person extricates himself from a certain way of life and saves himself from his past in order to reach another level of being.

The second level of repentance is the one in which deliberate sins are transmuted into virtues, when every transgression one has committed is reckoned as though it were a *mitzvah.*

To reach this very high level of repentance, an individual must change the very essence of himself so drastically that all the facts of his existence, all thoughts or actions, assume an entirely different meaning. He shifts into another field of being.

The incalculable difficulty of such a shift may be illustrated with a simple example from the physical world.

Let us take the laws of symmetry. While it is mathematically possible to find the correspondence for almost anything in terms of geometrical perspective, it is practically impossible to transform something with a right-hand symmetry to a left-hand symmetry, like a glove, for instance.

The whole system of coordinates has to be revolutionized or transcended.

To transform one's sins into virtues requires the same sort of total upheaval as changing a left glove to a right glove.

The shock of *teshuvah*

My father was an ardent socialist, almost a communist.

Once I visited the places in Spain where he fought in the civil war as a volunteer in the International Brigade.

I read Lenin before I read the Bible. It wasn't very fashionable when I became an Orthodox Jew. Nor was it easy.

I felt like the character in the Kafka novel who wakes up one day and discovers that he has become a cockroach.

I had always despised those Orthodox people. I really disliked them. I used to throw stones at them.

And then one day I woke up and discovered that I belonged there.

It was a shock. I don't know if I have ever really gotten over that shock.

The chart of human progress is not simple

There is the story of the Hasid who reached the next world and was asked what he wanted.

"Now," he said, "all I want is to enjoy being with God."

He was granted his wish, but nothing much came of it. Whereas if he had been a real saint (*tzaddik*), he would have said, "I wish for nothing more than to be nullified in God, to become nothing in Him."

Had he renounced his wish for the personal enjoyment of endless bliss, he would have been raised to a higher level of being.

The chart of human progress is not at all simple. Besides the contradictions hinted at, there are processes of cyclic formation, to and fro movements of development, and inner and outer metaphysical systems with great power to influence personality and transform it.

What is more, situations exist when a person is confronted with another sort of dilemma entirely, when the only thing to be done is to turn the situation inside out as one pulls open a glove.

Knowledge of one's sins can result in a transformation

While one person may need to make greater and more intense efforts toward Divine unity, another may desire no more than to be able to make an honest living.

There is also a matter of proportion.

The more one has been sunk in sin, the greater the pressure to emerge. Just as a dam holds back a body of water, the higher the dam, the greater is the power that can afterward be extracted from the release.

All of this means that the sinner has to go through the intervening stages of growth and comprehension.

The more he learns of the magnitude of his past transgressions, the more painful is the knowledge and the more effective is the transformation.

Three stages of spiritual development

If we translate historical events into terms pertaining to each individual's pilgrimage toward his true goal in life, the Promised Land, then the three festivals, together with their natural, agricultural symbolism of spring (Passover), reaping (Shavuot), and harvest (Sukkot), can be seen as landmarks along that path.

The individual journey begins when a person tears himself away from the state of aimlessness. This is the first step.

At this point, everything is still in the embryonic stage, incomplete and undefined—the festival of spring.

Clearly, at this stage, one does not fully understand the significance and future consequences of the spontaneous first step into the unknown.

Only later does one reach a degree of maturity and self-knowledge that gives an understanding of the road taken.

This is the time of the receiving of Torah, the feast of reaping.

And only long after, possibly many years later, does one reach full awareness and the ability to enjoy the good fruits.

This is the tranquil hour of the "season of our joy"—the feast of harvest.

These three stages of spiritual development can be found, in various forms, in the life of every individual, as well as in the spiritual and historical course of the nation as a whole.

Transforming one's sinful deeds into something meritorious

The highest level of repentance is the transformation of one's sinful deeds, making them accomplish something meritorious by changing the course of their consequences.

To a degree, the significance of an action may be measured not only by its intrinsic morality but also by its ultimate consequences.

This is a very high level and belongs to the way of holiness.

Where a person can effect such transformation of his sins, it becomes a powerful level, raising him to heights otherwise unattainable.

Our goal is always to aim for greater heights

It is taught that Rabbi Levi Yitzchak of Berditchev was unable to lead the prayer service one Yom Kippur. His Hasidim pleaded with him, to no avail.

"Last year," he told them, "I promised God I would do complete *teshuvah*. And look, the year passed by, and I still haven't repented. How can I possibly lead the prayers again?"

Finally, his son said to him, "Father, last year it wasn't true, but this time it will be!" Upon hearing those words, the rabbi took heart and began the prayers.

Cultivating the self-awareness necessary for *teshuvah* is an incremental process. Part of this process is acknowledging that we may not have lived up to our goals or promises from last year—or if we have indeed made progress, that last year's *teshuvah* does not suffice from our new vantage point.

Who we are now is different from who we were when we repented last year.

If I did not fulfill last year's promise, that does not contradict my ability now to promise sincerely.

What is important is not what has happened—or did not happen—in the past but whether or not a person is prepared to accept it, learn from it, and go forward. If we are not prepared to accept our past, including our sins and our suffering, it will come back repeatedly.

The Baal Shem Tov said that the penitent has the possibility of repentance when he is on a higher level of consciousness than he was at the time of the sin.

The sign of real development is that one's previous level no longer holds true for him.

When one genuinely grows, his personal truth now must surpass all his previous truths, so that by comparison, they are not true at all.

Teshuvah demands that one pursue one's individual truth at all times. Yesterday's heavens should be today's earth, and we must know: there is a Truth still higher than this.

Our goal is always to aim for greater heights, to be constantly struggling and striving to do better and to be closer to God.

It is not enough just to be.

One's life as an annex of the Holy Temple

One generally has a pretty good idea of what one is. The famous statement by Hillel reflects this: "If I am not for myself, who is for me, and if I am for myself, what am I?"

One's nothingness is not so hard to recognize.

What is hard is to reconcile it with one's potential for being a dwelling place for the *Shekhinah,* the Divine presence.

Every man is a contradiction in this sense, a combination of the holy and the trivial.

One has to integrate it all into some sort of workable unity by building one's life as though it were an annex in the court of the Holy Temple, the inner chambers of which one can never be sure of entering.

The chief work of man is to make corrections

Given the creation by God of a complete universe, it is a basic assumption that everything is interconnected.

One can see something like this by looking at drops of water. One sees reflections, smaller ones and bigger ones, like a house of mirrors—the same thing, the same nature, reflected in different ways.

It follows that if I would know perfectly, completely, entirely, one part, then I would know the whole. It is a beautiful thing.

When God says, "Let us make man," He is calling to the whole universe: "Let us make man." And each contributes something: the foxes and the lions, the monkeys and the angels—all give something.

So we are the result of everything that is.

The idea is that we contain—and this point is essential—the mind-body point of connection. The same hierarchy that exists in the body exists in the mind.

One of the ways to explain the basic concept of our religion is to say that because we are men, we have to connect.

We have free will, and we have the ability to repair. Because we have free will, we are also the only ones who have the ability to distort.

One of our problems is that of choice. There is an attempt to become better. It is like making corrections for a lens.

The lens becomes not right for some reason, so it distorts whatever is seen through it.

We believe that the main duty, the chief work, of man is to make corrections until it is possible to transmit the right picture.

Using a certain skill of a wrestler

When one has extraneous thoughts, instead of feeling despair, one has to resort to a certain wrestler's skill, using the weight of the opponent to topple him and then slipping from under his grip by an ingenious clarity of purpose and will.

As Rabbi Schneur Zalman of Liadi, the Baal haTanya, says, there are two souls waging war against each other in a person's mind. And the prize for which they are fighting is the individual's progress toward God.

In Judaism, children were never considered little angels

Judaism never looked on children as innocent and pure. They were never considered little angels.

On the contrary, they were considered liable to sin and act cruelly out of ignorance.

Man is not born human. He comes into the world as a wild young creature. As he grows, he may become tame.

His wildness as a child is a result of not grasping the existence of the other; it is ignorance, a lack of knowledge that makes empathy impossible.

Walking the path to infinity

A person who is in a state of repentance throughout his life is not someone who must atone for a particular sin.

He is someone who is returning to God, to the source and root of his soul.

He is coming ever closer and growing ever more intimately connected to Him.

He is walking on a path that reaches to infinity, a path without end on which he walks forever, in a state of repentance throughout his life.

We do *teshuvah* in a universe that transcends physical laws

The urge to repent grows out of the realization that it is necessary to change.

Lamenting our past wrongdoing will not serve us, for contact with evil is inescapable.

We must avoid pondering the past and reliving it as it happened, complete with faults and mistakes.

Rather, we should meditate on it, as it ought to have been. The main thrust of *teshuvah* is not only to redeem but also to rebuild the past.

But here we must address a looming epistemological obstacle. Because time is strictly unidirectional, we cannot revert to some previous moment.

As a result, our efforts to engage in *teshuvah* are at best paradoxical.

We must remember that we do not undertake *teshuvah* in a conventional universe.

We do *teshuvah* in a universe that transcends physical laws—a universe in which the present, the future, and the past merge into a timeless continuum, a universe in which a lethal arrow can fly back into its quiver and be as free of suspicion as if it had never left.

Teshuvah transports us into a state of weightlessness, where opposing polarities, of plus and minus, reverse at will and standard metrics are suspended.

To enter this state, we will have to truly know ourselves. And if our goal is not just to repent but to accomplish an about-face, our challenge will be still greater, for we will have to reach the innermost depths of our being, the nadir of the abyss, as it were.

In this realm, we are entitled to believe that our souls are not far from God.

Unless we reach this zone, we cannot be convinced that a radical change has taken place deep down in our hearts, a change that is capable of transcending all the rules of the universe.

It's easy to fool oneself

There once was a famous recluse and ascetic who was also a great scholar and something of a saint. He wore sackcloth and practiced self-denial.

One day, he went to visit one of the great Hasidic rabbis. When he arrived, he thought it would be appropriate to open his jacket a little and expose the sackcloth underneath.

The rabbi peered at him and kept saying, "How clever he is! How wise he is!"

The ascetic could not refrain from asking, "Who? Who is wise?"

And the rabbi answered, "The Evil Impulse—who took someone like you and put him into a sack."

The truth is that all one's life, one can remain modest and frugal and still be doing it entirely for oneself.

CHAPTER 11

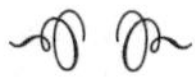

The Pursuit of Happiness

"A person is weighed in the balance not by the peace of mind he attained but rather by the nature of his struggle and what was won in the battle."

The quest is not for peace of mind

The question is asked about the universal longing and aspiration for peace of mind and heart. There are those who do not reach too high a degree of tranquillity.

It is taught that God weighs every person differently. Some are judged according to their achievements and others by their failures.

A person is weighed in the balance not by the peace of mind he attained but rather by the nature of his struggle and what was won in the battle.

Great happiness is not the goal of life

There is a story of a Hasid who was very poor and yet somehow acquired a set of fine ritual utensils for the Passover seder.

With his whole soul uplifted, he arranged each of the objects and happily performed the seder ceremony, giving it the utmost feeling and devotion and, indeed, experiencing a feeling that he was transported into higher spheres.

The seder continued late into the night.

The next day, he was barely able to rest and prepare himself to perform the second seder.

He was so rushed and preoccupied that he felt none of the enthusiasm of the previous day and was afterward quite depressed.

Some days later, he went to the rabbi, who looked at him pointedly and told him, "At Pesach, one of my disciples had a Heavenly feeling on the evening of the first seder. He felt uplifted—so what? But the second seder, that was very, very good."

In other words, the feeling of great happiness or sublimity is not in itself of any consequence.

To be truly free

Freedom and slavery appear to be simple opposites, each defined as the absence of the other: slavery, the absence of freedom; freedom, the absence of slavery.

But each of these terms must be understood without reference to the other.

Throwing off one's fetters does not necessarily mean that one has entered into a state of freedom.

Slavery is that condition in which a person is always subject to the will of another.

Freedom, on the other hand, is the ability to act on, and carry out, one's own independent will.

The individual who lacks a will of his own does not become free once he is unshackled.

He is simply a slave without a master, or, in the case of a people, those whose overlords have abandoned them.

Between ceasing to be a slave and acquiring freedom, the individual must thus pass through an intermediate stage in his progress, without which he cannot become truly free. He must develop inner qualities of his own.

The miracle of the Exodus was not completed with the people's departure from the house of bondage.

They needed to develop to become a truly free people and not merely runaway slaves.

Spiritually free

The meaning of the word "exile" is not limited to a physical definition.

As with slavery, the meaning and full significance of the word lies in the spiritual realm.

To be in exile means that one has surrendered oneself to a set of values, relationships, and a way of life that are foreign to the individual or collective ego.

When the persecuted Jewish people went into exile, they had to change their mode of living and the ways in which they sustained themselves.

Once an agricultural people, they now turned to trade and commerce; once free and independent, they were now subject to various lords; once the masters of their own way of life, they now had to sway with every passing breeze.

As long as they retained their independent spiritual character, their religious principles, their internal leadership, and their distinctive way of life, the Jewish people were never truly enslaved—at least not in the spiritual dimension of their existence.

The elementary meaning of freedom

The Exodus was the casting off of the yoke of slavery.

But in and of itself, the Exodus did not grant freedom.

Freedom is more than the mere casting off of bondage. Freedom also has a positive meaning.

Slavery and bondage are states in which both an individual and a nation are not free to do what their hearts desire but are constrained to do what others tell them to do.

A state of freedom exists only when a person can do what he wants and can live his own life.

This, of course, cannot be achieved unless he has a will of his own and an intrinsic direction to his life. This point applies not only to human beings or to specific interpretations of the concept of freedom.

It is, in fact, the elementary meaning of freedom. Freedom without an independent will has no essence and therefore makes no sense.

To be free means to have a life goal of one's own

It is a well-known phenomenon that animals born and raised in captivity who escape from their cages often do not know how to live in freedom.

They are not capable of taking care of themselves, nor do they have the motivation.

When in their cages, they look as if they are constantly striving to set themselves free, acting out of a vague instinct.

When they do attain freedom, it usually takes them no more than a few days to return to the comfort of their pen, with its well-known routine and attendant—even if that attendant makes them work.

And if this is true for animals, it is much truer for human beings.

For to be free means to have a personality of one's own, to have a life goal of one's own, a goal that is worth striving for despite all difficulties.

PART III

The Children of Israel

"What we are is a family. We are the biological or, in the case of converts, the spiritual children of the House of Israel. We are connected to one another, whether or not we agree with one another, whether or not we even like one another."

CHAPTER 12

What Does It Mean to Be Jewish?

"Being a Jew means that God intervenes in our pocketbooks, in our kitchens, in our bedrooms."

The Jews, as a people, are obsessed with God

The mission of the Jews? We are priests.

As priests, we have a special mission.

There is a difference between a priest and a pastor. A pastor is a person who has to be a teacher, a leader.

And contrary to what many people may say, I don't think that being a light unto the nations means that we are the teachers of the world.

In any case, the world doesn't like our teachings.

The role of the priest is, first of all, that the priest accepts a great number of special duties. But as priests, we are, basically, a people, obsessed with God.

We are all obsessed with Him.

That is, perhaps, another definition of what a Jew is: a person who is obsessed with God.

It is almost impossible for us to live without worshiping our God.

Now, the problem is, what is the function of the priest who is a nonreligious person?

Being a priest is so essential to our being that if we lose our God, we try to invent a new one as fast as possible in order to do something that is in our nature—that is, to be priests.

The uniting element is undeniably there

Even though at times we may think that we have nothing in common, as happens in every normal family, the people in the Jewish family have all kinds of ties and links that are enormously hard for us to explain.

We somehow find ourselves at ease with each other. Despite the occasional infighting, we are comfortable within our own family.

Understandably, too, we feel a certain amount of safety in being together, and we find it easier to make connections within the family.

But of course, brothers and sisters tend to get estranged. They move to different countries and adopt different accents, ways of life, ways of behavior.

Nevertheless, this uniting element remains.

It is very primitive, very hard to define, but undeniably there.

Defining a Jewish community

There is a story in the Talmud of a man who went to Babylon and had reason to ask for some help with something.

The Jews there did not come to his assistance, with money or anything else. The man, in describing them, wrote that these were evidently not Jews but a mongrel community, because they failed to show kindness.

He did not inquire whether they prayed or put on *tefillin* or wore *tzitzit.* The fact that they did not act naturally and spontaneously with kindness was decisive.

We Jews are optimists

There is a quotation from the Kabbalistic work of Rabbi Chaim Vital, *Sefer Etz Chayyim,* that our world is one that in its majority is a world of evil. Evil is the ruler of this world, and there is very little good in it.

If I could express it in perhaps a paradoxical way, I would turn to the eighteenth-century dispute between Leibniz and Voltaire.

Leibniz said we lived in the best of all possible worlds, and Voltaire, who wrote *Candide,* made fun of Leibniz and came to the conclusion that we live in the worst of all possible worlds.

If we were to look at this question from a Jewish point of view, I would answer in the following way: "We are living in the worst of all possible worlds in which there is still hope."

There are, indeed, worlds below us in which there is no hope at all, and this is what we call "Hell."

But to speak of the entire structure of our own world, it really is a world on the very brink.

If it were to be slightly, just slightly, worse than it actually is, then its basic structure would become entirely hopeless.

The balance would be irreversible, and evil would be irrevocable.

As it is now, evil can be conquered, but we are not living in a Leibnizian paradise.

Rather, we live in a world in which we have to accept a vast amount of evil.

What I am saying is not usually understood as a Jewish idea, but I think that it is really a statement of what I would call "Jewish optimism."

If a person sees the world as all pink and glowing, he is not an optimist; he's just a plain fool.

An optimist, on the other hand, is one who, in spite of seeing the terrible facts as they are, believes that there can be improvement.

If everything were all right, then you wouldn't have to be an optimist. So I do believe that we, as Jews, are optimists because we are a people with hope and we have a theology of hope.

A real Jew would rather die than worship idols

Thirty years ago, I taught a class on the issue of who is a Jew. We said then that a real Jew is one who would choose to sanctify God's Name and even die for the choice, rather than worship idols.

Jewish history is replete with thousands of examples, not only of righteous people but also of simple Jews who died for the sanctification of God's Name.

In a sense, the Jewish people is just as proud of its thieves and prostitutes who died for the sanctification of God's Name as it is of its rabbis and righteous ones.

It is the thieves and prostitutes who attest most to the existence of that inner core, independent of tradition or erudition, which is the very essence of being a Jew.

I asked the class whether they thought this definition was still valid. At that point, the question was left hanging.

The next day, I flew to a kibbutz near Eilat and spoke there.

I do not remember exactly what I said, but I do remember that I managed to make my listeners furious.

At some point, one man, who could no longer contain himself, got up and screamed, "I am a secular Jew, and so were my father and grandfather. But I am telling you, if someone would force me to worship idols, I would die rather than do it."

This was almost like a voice from Heaven.

I received the answer some twenty-four hours after having been asked the question, and not from someone who heard it, but rather from someone who innocently, in a moment of rage, answered exactly the question that I had asked.

What is it that we are so eager to pass on?

There is much concern about continuity in the Jewish world today.

Achieving continuity is not an end in itself, however.

We must be concerned not only with how to ensure continuity but also why.

What is it that we are so eager to pass on?

Jewish continuity is a centuries-long relay, in which the "baton" is some manifestation of our special relationship with God.

Abraham and Sarah passed the tradition on to Isaac, and he and Rebecca passed it on to Jacob.

And just as the upcoming runner strides in tandem with his predecessor before the latter completely relinquishes the baton, so, too, each of us, ideally, has the opportunity to share our understanding and appreciation of our tradition with our offspring, before entrusting them to continue the journey.

The Jews are a stiff-necked people

When the Jews, immediately after receiving the Torah, made the Golden Calf, Moses prayed to God, asking Him to forgive the people for this terrible sin. He said, "For it is a stiff-necked people, and You shall forgive."

This seems strange. If they are obstinate people, why should God forgive them?

The Ramban, Rabbi Moses ben Nachman, who lived in the thirteenth century in Spain, answered this question. He wrote that the verse means that Moses says to God:

"You know your people. They are a terribly obstinate people. To move them from one level to another, from one position to another, takes a long time. Because of this, you should forgive them.

"You must remember that they lived four hundred years amid an evil nation. You want them to change? You can't expect them to change in a day. It will take them years and years to change.

"But when they are changed, the same obstinacy will be on your side. They will never leave you."

Being Jewish means we have obligations

José Ortega y Gasset, a Spanish philosopher and sociologist, wrote a book titled *The Revolt of the Masses* in which he says that nobility is best expressed by the French expression *noblesse oblige,* nobility obligates.

Nobility is not about rights or riches. It's about obligations.

The higher someone's noble rank, the more obligations one has.

Being Jewish means that we have obligations from the moment we open our eyes to the moment we go to sleep, from the day we are born to the day we are buried.

They never leave us, not for one moment.

There is no time in which we can say, "OK, dear God, now we'll part ways. We'll meet again sometime."

Being a Jew means that God intervenes in our pocketbooks, in our kitchens, in our bedrooms.

It doesn't mean that we're not allowed to do anything.

We're allowed to do lots of things—but always with the notion that Somebody is there, and He's keeping track.

The concept of Israel means me

In terms of responsibility to God and doing His will through *mitzvot,* the concept of Israel means, first of all, me.

When one recites in prayer, "Who chooses His people Israel with love," one is thinking not of the chief rabbi but of oneself.

When one says, "You alone will we worship with awe and reverence," one is also thinking not of any official body at the head of the community but, again, of oneself.

In other words, when one says "we" in this context, or "we Jews," or "we, the people of Israel," one means "I," or at least primarily "I."

As it was once expressed by a *tzaddik,* "A person should pray in the synagogue as though he were in a forest, with a tree here and a tree there, and feel that he alone is communicating with God in worship."

The only way we can really know ourselves

The law of entropy is found in every physical part of the world, according to which all things must run down.

The world tends to a state of decreased order. Everything runs down and eventually crumbles.

Within the cosmos, in which the law of entropy holds sway, there is also the realm of biology.

Even though the biological realm is contained in the general physical-chemical laws, it includes a pulling in the opposite direction. Every living thing grows up, develops, and becomes bigger and more complicated.

I am trying not to explain these contradictions but to state the fact that while a general rule applies to most things, a particular, seemingly contradictory rule applies to a part of them.

We have to understand our special history within world history analogously.

The laws of growth, development, and decay that apply to other cultures do not apply to our people.

Their times of greatness, and their ideas of greatness, did not coincide with ours.

Understanding this difference, and trying to identify with it, is the only way we can really know ourselves.

CHAPTER 13

The Jewish Family

"We have our own approach to all sorts of matters."

We are a family

Jews can hardly be categorized as a nation.

We cannot even be considered a religion in the ordinary sense of a religion with a message that we think should become general, that we want to sell to others.

All together, we are a very different sort of entity.

To clarify what we are, we may start by saying that we are a family, just a family.

We are a large one, not entirely a biological one, but basically a family.

A family tie, sociologically speaking, is far more basic than that of either a nation or a religion.

The family tie is a very primitive way of binding people, but it is probably the most stable one, and the most resistant to outside change and influence.

We are not a perfect family, but we are a real family

What does it mean to identify oneself as a Jew?

As a rabbi, as someone who is, one might say, a Jew by profession, I have given a fair amount of thought to this issue.

The most obvious first answer, I believe, is that a person is a Jew by religion.

In fact, that is a hard argument to make, as odd as it may seem. There is no basic set of meaningful principles on which all Jews would agree. And there are huge variations in both practice and belief.

Are Jews members of a race? This is clearly not the case. Jews come in every color and exhibit every combination of ethnic features.

Do Jews belong to a nation? Following the involuntary exile inflicted on us many centuries ago, the notion of Jews as a people living in one place, speaking one language, or even sharing one culture does not fit.

Even linguistically, we are splintered. Hebrew is our official language, the language of the land of Israel and of our sacred texts, but many Jews have no knowledge of it at all.

What we are is a family. We are the biological or, in the case of converts, the spiritual children of the House of Israel.

We are connected to one another, whether or not we agree with one another, whether or not we even like one another.

We are not a perfect family, but we are a real family. We are all proud when one of us does well and embarrassed when one of us does badly. And as much as we may argue among ourselves, we are always there to defend or assist one another.

The connection is beyond choice

Judaism as a religion was never very active in proselytizing, just as a family would never go out into the streets to grab people to join the family.

It doesn't mean that Jews feel superior or inferior. It's simply that from the very beginning, Judaism had its own rhythm and way of living.

Even when members of such a family are out of the family house, when they are wandering far away, they continue the lifestyle—theologically, sociologically, behavioristically.

Of course, members of the family can be severely chastised, and rifts can occur between individuals and groups, but there is really no way of leaving the family.

You can even hate it, but you cannot be separated from it.

After some time, people, younger or older, come to the conclusion that they can't get away from it, and therefore it is far better to try to find the ways in which they are connected—because the connection is beyond choice.

It's a matter of being born with it. And since you are stuck with it, it is far better to get to know where you came from and who you are.

Finding out to which family one belongs

For some of our people, it's almost like the story of the duckling that was hatched by a hen.

Too often, our ducklings grow up in a different atmosphere. They are taught to think and act in ways that are entirely alien.

Jews have adopted a lot of other cultures, national identities, and sometimes even religions. Sometimes a wonderful recognition and return occurs.

Frequently, however, it takes the form of a very unpleasant discovery that "I am somehow different," that "my medium is a different medium."

When a Jew finds water, so to speak, he will swim in it, even though those who raised him and taught him don't.

Finding out somehow to which family one belongs is a familiar theme in literature, and in life, knowingly or unknowingly, each person begins to discover it.

If the discovery comes soon enough, the person is not only able to acknowledge the fact that he belongs somewhere—at least to be buried in the right graveyard—but also to make his life, in a way, more sensible.

Paradoxically, freedom comes with the acceptance of a definite framework from which one cannot move away.

Judaism is the way we as a family move

Judaism, as a religion, is simply the way of our particular family. It is the way we do certain things.

We walk and talk with God and man, like everyone else, but we have our own way of doing these things.

As in any other family, we try sometimes, when we are young, to run away, to fight our parents. Later on in life, we find ourselves resembling them more and more.

This particular way, which is called Judaism, is in many respects the way that we as a family move together—pray, dress, eat, do a variety of things.

We have our own approach to all sorts of matters. For example, in our family, we don't eat certain things.

This doesn't mean that we make a special claim of any kind, saying, "We are the best family there is."

But as in any group of people, we may have this feeling, and nobody can blame us.

Telling myself that "my father is different" or "my brother is different" is very human.

The truth of being home

One can point to more beautiful mansions and more exciting sites, but these can never replace one's home.

Like any personal roaming and wandering of individuals separated from their family, the desperate attempt to be independent only leads to a discovery that somewhere along the line, one must try to come back and find the truth of being home.

Israel is an entity

Israel, taken as a whole, is an entity, with feet and toenails, chest and head, and soul.

To a degree, the rest of the body receives life and power from the consciousness in the head.

And the heads of Israel are the souls of men like the *tzaddikim,* who are able to be in some kind of contact both with God and with the people.

It was said of a famous Hasid that if a woman was in labor within five hundred miles of him, he was unable to sleep because of the pain.

Can a head be real if it does not sense every ache of the body?

The definition of a Jew is beyond biology

It may be pertinent to point out a few important basic Jewish concepts that have become obscured as a result of the long controversy with Christianity and the defensive measures that had to be taken.

In ancient times, the scholar of the Torah was not just an ordinary person with a gift for intellectual matters.

He was considered a sort of repository of holiness.

The implication of such an idea was that the Torah scholar, the *talmid chakham,* is like a temple or an altar to which one offers gifts.

To support and sustain him is a religious duty.

The idea that the patriarchs are the *merkavah*, the Chariot, implies that they unite, almost physically, with the essence of the Divine so that holiness passes through them biologically, strange as this may seem.

This means that the Divine spark is transferred to their descendants, irrespective of other facts.

A Jew, therefore, was one who had this holiness in him; and if he decided to convert out of Judaism, it was a sign that he wasn't really a Jew in essence, even though he may have been born of Jewish parents.

Similarly, a Gentile who became a proselyte was really a Jew in essence, even though he may not have been born of Jewish parents.

The definition of who is a Jew is thus clearly beyond biology; it is simply one who has the holy spark.

And according to the Baal haTanya, the confirmation of this definition resides in the fact that in the last resort, when facing some ultimate decision such as martyrdom, the Jew will offer himself to God.

O Guardian of Israel, protect the remnant of Israel

This feeling that "time is short," as stated in *Pirkei Avot,* is what spurs me on in whatever I do, in my attempts to infect others with the feeling of how short time is and how it is becoming shorter and shorter.

People criticize me, saying that I do too many different things. But in fact, I am doing one thing only—I am trying to be a partner in what it says in one of the prayers: "O Guardian of Israel, protect the remnant of Israel: . . . those who proclaim '*Shema Yisrael*'—'Hear, O Israel.' "

I want to ensure that the existence of the Jewish people be a meaningful one, in which *Shema Yisrael* can continue to be said. This may not be a great dream, but there is enough work here for an entire generation.

And I can see not only the agitation and the constant changes that are happening in the world in general and in the Jewish world in particular but also the lack of awareness of how short time is and what a great difference the work of a few years can make right now.

CHAPTER 14

The Jewish Family in Jeopardy

"We cannot live in the past, and we cannot live through others. Life is not a vicarious activity."

We are bleeding with smiles on our faces

It seems that the Jewish people have chosen a method of self-destruction somewhat reminiscent of an ancient Roman custom.

How did people commit suicide in ancient Rome? A person would get inside a warm bath and cut his own veins. Then he would sit there and bleed with a smile on his face, quietly, peacefully, unto death.

This is what is happening to the Jewish people nowadays.

There is a constant bleeding, not dramatic, but ongoing and unceasing.

We will need a memorial for the Jews we lose through assimilation

If things continue the way they are, there will be a need not only for a memorial foundation for the Jews who were killed in the Holocaust but also for a greater memorial foundation for the Jews whom we lose through assimilation.

We once lost part of our people through genocide, but at least we knew how to fight against the world's hostility.

But we are as yet quite unable to deal with the world's "love" and to regain what we lose through it.

Jewish education is so lacking that it almost has no meaning

There are many Jews whose only sense of being Jewish is the sense that they are hated, that they are a persecuted minority.

But when Judaism is defined solely as a kick in the pants, it's not worth continuing.

The root of the problem is that Jewish education, almost all over the world, is so lacking that it almost has no meaning.

To use an example from the physical sciences, in flight mechanics, there is what is called a critical velocity, under which no plane will fly.

Similarly, there is a critical level of Jewish knowledge under which no effective tie with Judaism will ever be reached.

Below this level, all attempts to teach Judaism are quite useless.

Kosher-centered Judaism

"Kosher-centered Judaism" is a Judaism that tries to fashion a small world in which you can feel Jewish through those things that are somehow obligations.

They have to be of a material nature—easy to see, easy to discuss, easy to solve—things that you can easily work at.

You can work at being kosher. You can buy another pair of *tefillin*.

I think this is an unhealthy sign—being kosher is only a part of being Jewish, as anybody who has any interest in Judaism knows.

It becomes some kind of routine, and people deal with this aspect because they are not interested in anything really important about Judaism.

I don't think that it can go on forever because it is boring, and after some time, it becomes boring even for those who participate in this sport.

It is just a shell, and the shell has no inner core.

I don't believe that it will survive.

Too long, too boring, and too frequent

When the Sabbath is treated as a weekend, with or without synagogue attendance, it feels like the secular weekend: too long, too boring, and too frequent.

When the Sabbath is not distinguished from the weekdays—set apart as a special time with a special mind-set—it is meaningless.

If we view the Sabbath candles as decorations, they will be superfluous.

If we light the candles in an effort to welcome holiness, however, they will give off a special radiance.

If we call up some friends to arrange the next golf outing, we will have just another weekend.

If we can connect our shared conversation at our Sabbath table with holiness, however, we will experience *oneg*, the delight that our tradition extols.

If we overload our day with too much food or too much empty chitchat, we will gain nothing.

But if we accept God's invitation to share His day with Him and allow a bit of the world to come to waft into our world, we will treasure life with a feeling of wholeness and contentment.

Jewish leaders don't even understand Jewish jokes

There is an immediate need for at least some schools to provide us with what we need most—Jewishly educated leadership and willing Jewish teachers at every level.

We need teachers, we need better textbooks, we need to create a knowledge corps that will disperse all over the Jewish world—to teach. We must teach abstract knowledge and the laws and the history and the language—the Jewish way of life.

This can yet be done. We have the people and the resources, and perhaps we still have some people who know the pressing need for it.

We have to re-create the Jewish audience, re-create the Jewish home.

We need schools for educating Jewish leaders so that they at least should know what the needs are.

We are coming to an age when Jewish leaders don't even understand Jewish jokes.

And this is a very bad thing. A Jewish joke is not part of the Jewish creed, but it is part of the Jewish heritage. And when there comes a generation that doesn't understand it, it's very bad for us.

The Jewish people must regain its own essence

The real tragedy of the exile in Egypt was that the slaves gradually became more and more like their masters, thinking like them and even dreaming the same dreams.

Their greatest sorrow, in fact, was that their masters would not let them fulfill the Egyptian dream.

It was not enough for them to realize how much they were suffering under the harsh regime to which they were subject—they had to decide that they no longer wanted any part of it.

To change the Egyptian class structure so that they, too, might aspire to become officers and overlords would not have sufficed to liberate them from their bondage.

Only when they were ready to depart not only from the physical land of Egypt but also from the conceptual world in which they had lived, when they were ready to sacrifice their devotion to

Egyptian values along with that first Paschal Lamb—only then could they truly be redeemed.

In order to achieve true redemption, and not only an end to exile, it is not enough for the Jewish people to leave "the wilderness of the nations."

It must regain its own essence, its character, spirit, ways of thinking, and ways of life.

Only then can it really be free.

Only then will it have been redeemed.

The destruction of the Holy Temple is a key to all of Israel's troubles

The destruction of the Holy Temple in Jerusalem constitutes both a key to and a definition of all of the troubles of Israel.

It is this destruction that lifts isolated events, persecutions, exiles, and oppressions from the plane of mere historical episodes and gives them a transcendent significance.

For the Jewish people, the Temple was the only place for complete worship. It was the recognized center for all the children of Israel, however scattered they were.

Indeed, the Temple was the only holy place recognized by Judaism.

The central importance of the Temple can only be fully appreciated by studying Maimonides' list of the *mitzvot.*

Of the 613 listed, fewer than half of them are applicable, and some of the others only partly so, following the Temple's destruction.

And the situation is similar in the Oral Law and in all the other areas that make up the life of the nation.

It may be said that much of the structure of Judaism was suddenly cut out from under it with the destruction, not only in activities directly connected with the Temple and the worship there but also a large body of *mitzvot* and customs indirectly bound to it.

This picture of the effect on Jewish law gives us some conception of what really occurred with the destruction of the Temple.

When we are not one, Israel is in a state of deprivation and suffering

The concept of *ahavat Yisrael,* the love of one's fellow Jews, points to the love of God.

One does not attain it by remaining in the material body and feeling all sorts of sentiments about one's brethren.

It is attained by striving for, and ultimately reaching, that level of being in which one sees oneself as a soul.

Consistent with this point of view, a rather extreme notion of Israel as a physical-spiritual collective body has developed over the centuries.

It is something so sensitively organic in its unity that any separation of one of its smallest limbs or parts was seen to inflict a serious injury on the whole, which was the *Shekhinah,* the Divine indwelling.

A common expression of this is reflected in the words of the blessing "Bless us all, our Father, as one, with the light of Thy countenance."

When we are all one, we can receive the light of "Thy countenance."

When we are not one, the Divine presence is not in its right place, and Israel is in a state of deprivation and suffering.

The destiny of the Jewish person who has been estranged

When animals brought up in a zoo are released, sometimes they do not even know whether they are wolves or deer.

They have to find out who they are, what they are.

It's a great discovery to learn "I am this" and to explore the right way of behavior for one's own kind.

Such is the destiny of a Jewish person who has been estranged.

He may or may not find helpers.

He may almost instinctively move into his natural habitat, or he may have all kinds of strange resistances that will interfere forever with his normal behavior, so that possibly it can be corrected only in a later generation.

Whatever happens, such a one is at least coming to grips with the problem.

Frequently, the process is accompanied by tragic mishaps—finding, losing, finding again.

But basically, it is the situation of the person who wakes up and finds out that even though he grew up somewhere in midwestern America, he really belongs to this very old family, with those strange parents, those sometimes lonely, sometimes ugly brothers and sisters.

He has to get accustomed to this idea and then find out what to do about it.

A symptom of the spiritual malady from which we are suffering

When the general knowledge of the Jewish intellectual is on the university level and his Jewish knowledge is on the grade-school level, his Jewish knowledge cannot compete, and it will always cause some kind of a rift and some degree of self-contempt.

It is not only a matter of learning Jewish studies but also of trying to see things Jewishly—in a thousand different ways.

When we speak about "Jewish myth," for example, and we discuss whether it is a good or a bad thing, this in itself shows that we accept the outlook of the world around us.

Indeed, we don't look at our history and life from our own point of view but from without, like strangers—and this is a symptom of the spiritual malady from which we are suffering.

Life is not a vicarious activity

Many Jews would say that the state of Israel is the answer to the unsolved problems of the Jews in the Diaspora.

If we just send our children to Israel to be "inoculated" against assimilation, we will not have to worry about Jewish continuity in the United States.

Israel is important—there is no question—but not everyone is going to Israel.

The Jews did not all return to Jerusalem when the Temple was rebuilt, and they are surely not all returning now.

Depending on Israel to save American (or Russian or European) Jewry is asking a lot; Israel has enough to do to save herself.

We cannot live in the past, and we cannot live through others. Life is not a vicarious activity.

Just as I cannot eat for someone else or sleep for someone else, I cannot study for someone else.

Life is something each of us must do on our own.

And if this is true of the mundane actions that keep my body alive, it is even more true of the exalted activities that nourish my spirit.

A blessing or a curse?

Our choice, as Jews, is not whether to remain Jews. Our choice is whether to take it as a curse or as a blessing.

This is our choice.

We don't have a choice about being or not being Jews. We have a choice about the way we accept it.

We can accept it as a curse, as lots of people accept a hereditary illness.

But even then, if it is a disease that has been in the family for generations, you want to find out about it.

If we are all suffering from one disease, we should at least properly explore it to understand what kind of disease it is.

PART IV

Torah

"Thousands of interpretations have already been written on Genesis, all trying to explain, reveal, and decipher the story—and still the secret remains inviolable, because the secret of the Torah is a real secret."

CHAPTER 15

The Nature of Torah

"It is like a secret code with an infinite number of possible interpretations, a tale within a tale within a tale."

The Torah comes to man across the abyss of the infinite

The efficacy of the Torah does not depend on the degree a person penetrates into its content or meaning or even on the purification of one's mind and actions in relation to the ethical ramifications of doing good or combating evil.

Even the social benefits, no matter how great, are incidental and peripheral.

The essential fact about the Torah is the way it comes to man, across the abyss of the infinite, as a communication of God's will, God's thought.

The more external reasons and justifications a person gives for living according to the Torah, the more scaffolding and superstructure he adds to the essential revelation.

There are many people who need these reasons, for a while or for all their lives. One circumcises one's son because it is hygienic or traditional, one eats kosher because it is healthy, and so forth.

No matter how subtle and sublime the rationalizations, it does not change the fact that ultimately, one is not doing the *mitzvah* because it is good or pleasant or beneficial but because God has said, "I want it."

Since one cannot establish a communication with God on one's own level, within the world one lives or in the language one understands, one has to use this code, this way of getting to Him as experienced in revelation.

This revelation does provide a certain system of words, actions, forms, and situations, namely, the *mitzvot* of the Torah.

This is the given area where contact can be made.

There are many ways to connect with the Torah

A single individual cannot be expected to carry out all the 613 *mitzvot* in the Torah.

For example, there are *mitzvot* that concern only a man or a woman, a priest or a king.

But a person can perform them as part of the whole of Israel, as an integral component of a particular generation in time and place. Every generation is a cross section of the timeless entity that is Israel.

Even if a person cannot carry out a *mitzvah* in terms of action, he can perform it in speech and in thought.

By reading aloud and studying the Torah, all 613 *mitzvot* find their expression in the individual's soul.

There are many levels of uniting with the Torah, depending on one's capacities.

There are those who are limited by their intellects. Others are limited by their willpower or their soul roots.

A person may comprehend something in Scripture and yet be unable to make contact with it because the root of his soul shrinks from it.

All people are conscious of an attraction to certain aspects of the Torah and an incapacity to react to others.

The Torah is like a tale within a tale within a tale

It is the very letters of the Torah, not only the sentences, that reveal God's will.

This is one of the characteristics of the Torah, differentiating it from other sacred works like the Mishnah. The holiness of the Torah is in the very letters of the text.

This makes for a difference in relation to the study of these books, as tradition has shown.

Every letter and sign in the Torah is pored over as a Divine mystery waiting to be revealed.

The combinations of the letters in words and sentences are the manner in which their meaning is communicated to us.

One may make all sorts of combinations, on a variety of levels, and obtain six hundred thousand possible revelations.

As the Ramban said, all of the Torah spells out the names of God. It is a list of His names, very little of which has any meaning for us.

It is like a secret code with an infinite number of possible interpretations, a tale within a tale within a tale.

Each one is equally valid and holy.

The Torah is always expanding

The blessing that is recited on the occasion of reading from the Torah scrolls, "Blessed art Thou . . . who gives us the Torah," is in the present tense, "gives," not the past, "gave."

The Torah itself is always forming and expanding.

It is a constant growth. The event at Mount Sinai is an ongoing revelation that repeats itself whenever one studies the Torah.

One may not be aware of standing before the holy mountain, but God is still uttering the Ten Commandments.

Even if one does not hear them, the standing itself, in awe and terror, is enough to establish the correct relationship to the Torah.

The realization of this is, in turn, something acquired by study.

The Torah descends so it can be grasped by mortals

A person can use the Torah as a bridge to God, although the Torah is not only an instrument. It is the Divine Wisdom.

It is the perfect vessel of communication between man and God.

The problem is that at the level of Divine Wisdom, the Torah is just as inaccessible as God Himself.

Therefore, the Torah has to descend, level by level, so that it can be grasped by ordinary mortals.

The Torah contains practical actions and specific instructions about life. Comparatively little is left to speculation of a higher level.

The Torah bows down to earth in order to enable all men to make contact with it.

As an illustration, consider the computer, composed as it is of a large number of levels.

At the highest levels, the theory and the details are so intricate that only the most expert minds can deal with it.

At lower levels, the people with normal education and intelligence can be taught to ask questions of the computer and receive answers.

The way in which the computer works is out of the range of those who operate it.

Similarly, were the Torah to remain at the level of the higher angels, it would be utterly incomprehensible.

But if it says that on Purim, one should give presents to the poor, the Torah becomes available to all men.

Even the whole realm of the abstract Law relating the Torah and action—why give presents to the poor, what this should consist of, and what if one is poor himself—all this is something an ordinary person need not concern himself with.

The one thing required is something that every man can do.

Such genuine contact is the start and basis.

Thereafter, the opportunity is given to all who care to enter the Torah to rise, level by level, to the infinite without ever losing this real contact.

Relating to the Torah for its own sake

God raised us to the level of consciousness in which we can participate in His *mitzvot* and in the accompanying Heavenly delight.

Such is the meaning of being occupied with the Torah for its own sake.

There are those who get involved with the Torah in order to imbibe its contents or to use it for whatever practical or even idealistic purpose they think best.

They are not relating to the Torah for its own sake.

That is for the love of the Torah itself and not for the benefits to be had from it.

To be occupied with the Torah for its own sake does not mean to relate to the Torah as a literary work or as moral instruction or even as wisdom but rather to let the Torah emanate its splendor and joy, to let it serve as a channel for Divine light.

The Torah's awesome power

If one were aware of the Torah's awesome power, it would hardly be possible to focus one's attention.

A man's dull-wittedness is often his protection, enabling him to relate to sacred texts without being consumed by them.

There is a tale that may illustrate this. A great king ordered the manufacture of a special crown, and he provided extremely valuable jewels and ornaments for this purpose.

The master jeweler prepared the frame, but when it came to setting the priceless jewels in their place, he found his hands trembling with anxiety lest something go wrong.

He called a local simple person, who had no idea of the value of the jewels, to put them in place, and the task was done simply, without any excitement.

In this way, too, an ordinary person who does not appreciate the terrible holiness of what he is doing may read the Torah and even determine halakhic procedure and ritual.

CHAPTER 16

Torah Study

"Why does God want us to study? Theologically, it is a way to commune with Him."

The study of Torah is weighed against all the commandments

It is possible for all men to study Torah and practice the *mitzvot.*

The *mitzvot* are practical actions that can be carried out in a definite time and place.

And this, in turn, fills all that is lacking in a person.

One can cultivate the well-tried habit of using all of one's free time to study Torah.

As it is written, Talmud Torah, the study of Torah, is weighed against all the other commandments in that it fills all the empty and unoccupied places, and it does not allow a person to be in a vacuum.

For there is no neutral territory. Either one is in the domain of the holy or one is abandoned to the other side.

Even when one is idle, walking in the field or whatever, the mind and heart are occupied with something or other.

This can be connected with Torah and things of the spirit, or it can be a surrender to temptation.

It doesn't matter on what level one studies

One of the most frequently misunderstood points about Torah study is the fact that intellectual achievement is not the purpose.

It does not matter how much or on what level one studies, whether it is mastery of all of the Talmud or reading a single psalm.

What matters is the purity of the relationship to the text and not the degree of intellectual comprehension.

It is the capacity to become a vessel of Torah.

All the levels are revealed

It is said that even if one studies Torah without knowledge of its esoteric meanings but does so "for the sake of Heaven," all the various levels of the Torah are revealed.

In Torah, there is no distortion or artificiality.

There is only a contraction of holiness into various molds.

When a person studies Torah, he creates an angel

When a person studies Torah, he creates an angel and becomes a creature that has connections with a higher order of existence.

Any attempt to picture this spiritual essence has its limitations. It is of an experiential order.

That is, it is something that happens.

The physical pronunciation of holy words is a reality that transforms, and the sanctified essence thus created is connected to the person who created it.

Being trapped by the metaphor

The human body is often used to express various metaphorical concepts.

When we say that *chesed* and *gevurah* may be charted on a diagram of the *sefirot* as right and left in terms of function, we do not mean to insinuate that *chesed* is like the right hand of God or that it has anything to do with the right hand of man.

It is a model of only limited homologous relations that has value only because it enables the mind to grasp certain truths.

Thus, too, many of the source incidents of the halakhah, as described in the Scriptures, are really only models.

A butting ox, an exposed pit, and the like are models of legal problems or rather of relations between litigants.

Unfortunately, too many of those who study Talmud find it hard to extricate themselves from the confines of the model.

In this case, as in all instances of being trapped by the metaphor, the model becomes something absurd.

It is the imagination that interferes.

One has to learn to function on two levels.

One is recognizing that the model helps us understand something, and the other, that it doesn't really express the thing itself.

This sort of intellectual difficulty is sometimes the chief obstacle in the way of certain cultures that seek to adapt themselves to a scientific approach.

They confuse the model with the original object, often as a result of a long tradition of idolatry, of failing to distinguish the instruments of Divinity from Divinity.

And the failure to free oneself from the model and to relate to the source is idolatry.

If Torah study is not for the sake of Heaven, it is no more than playing

When a person makes something of himself and does not nullify himself before the Torah, his learning is of little consequence. If Torah study is not for the sake of Heaven, it is no more than playing.

Like those who claim that Torah study sharpens the mind.

Might they not better play chess or use something else to whet the brain?

That which does not repudiate itself before holiness cannot receive anything from it.

The effect of sanctity is to go out of oneself toward the other; I no longer want anything for myself.

The self is relinquished and abandoned.

The result is a spontaneous giving; the holy is always dealing out and bestowing gifts because it is not considering itself.

In contrast is an act of charity that is done, even if with the best of intentions, only because it makes one feel good.

The shell is easily capable of identifying with an image of righteousness that enhances the self.

To be sure, there are many degrees of such egotism, from the self-absorbed student to one who snatches what he can or just opens his mouth to be fed while presenting a show of clean hands.

The proper relation to Scripture

There is no essential difference between the one who studies with the highest esoteric comprehension and the one who merely reads the written words correctly.

To help illuminate this point, consider a complex electrical device.

Although one may not understand how it works, it may be easily operated by pushing certain buttons.

One simply has to be aware of the consequences of pressing the wrong one.

Although one may be limited in one's comprehension, there is no relation to the rightness or wrongness of what one does or to the benefit one gets from it.

So it is with Torah and halakhah—one may grasp more or less of the inner meaning and rise to higher levels according to one's ability.

This does not influence the degree of correctness of the action or the advantages of a proper relation to Scripture.

Each of us has the ability to "channel" God

The Torah is not a textbook.

If a textbook is objectively good, I may study from it, but how I relate to it is irrelevant.

I cannot argue with the mathematics it presents. I cannot argue with the rules of grammar it lays out.

Certainly, I can learn from it, but it is not important to me, because it is utterly independent of me.

It says what it says.

With the Torah, on the other hand, I have to find my message.

I have to figure out our relationship.

Therefore, I have to care.

I cannot glide over the text. I have to engage it.

But how do I prepare myself to receive the unique message God's Torah has for me? How do I get ready to convene with God?

According to Rabbi Schneur Zalman of Liadi, the eighteenth-century mystic and Talmudist, the precondition for this meeting is what he calls "self-nullification."

As developed in the *Tanya*, his quietly revolutionary work, self-nullification requires a person to separate from his ego, his smugness, and his importance.

This is not to denigrate the ego.

We need our egos in order to grow, in order to fulfill the biblical charge to master the world, in order to effect *tikkun olam.*

But just as we suspend our physical creativity, the tangible expression of our ego, on Shabbat and *yom tov,* we must also subordinate our egos, on the deepest level, during those activities in which we seek to join our will to God's.

A judge, for example, acting as an emissary of God in the search for truth and justice, must put aside his feelings, personal and philosophical, in order to adjudicate fairly.

He cannot disregard the facts and side with a poor petitioner over a wealthy one because he feels the wealthy one can better "afford" to lose. He must decide according to the law.

Similarly, a prophet can only prophesy when he transcends himself and becomes a conduit for God's words.

As we read in 2 Kings (3:11–15), when Elisha becomes angry, that is, when his ego is engaged, he cannot prophesy.

One need not be in a position as exalted as judge or prophet, however, to become a vessel through which God enters the world. 2 Samuel (6:14) relates how King David dances with utter abandon as he welcomes the Holy Ark back to Jerusalem.

Temporarily casting off his ego identities—of king, conqueror, and poet—and perhaps even his modesty, he is open to God, and God's approval is clear.

David's wife, who reprimands him for his lack of "dignity," is severely punished.

Each of us also has the ability to "channel" God. When we forget ourselves in prayer, we let God enter.

When we give *tzedakah,* not as an expression of our power but as an agent of God in the distribution of His bounty, we are God's conduit into the world.

And when we learn Torah as a way of unifying our minds with His, we are increasing God's presence on earth.

Participating in the Divine planning process

The range of Torah is much wider than what is outlined by human action. One is connected with the Divine will through the idea.

If, for instance, one studies a passage concerning a hypothetical circumstance, something that could never happen, the halakhic conclusion helps us know the Divine preference in any such situation.

In Torah study, one is engaged in the planning process.

It is in the planning or conceptualizing that there is a greater degree of participation in God.

What is more, by creating something new, man is able to expand this participation and to manifest God's will.

When we study Scripture, God studies with us

In *Pirkei Avot* ("Sayings of the Fathers"), a well-known tractate of the Mishnah, there is a statement to the effect that one hour of happiness in the world to come is better than all the life of this world.

Such a belief may satisfy the mystical ardor of many religious people.

But this statement is followed by a baffling statement that is opposite to the first—declaring that one hour of *teshuvah* (repentance) and *ma'asim tovim* (good deeds) in this world is worth more than all the life in the world to come.

In this world, we have something no other world contains.

We can come into direct communion with God through his Torah.

When we study Scripture, God studies with us, the Talmud says. When we perform actions according to the Torah, we are not separate from Him.

Why does God want us to study?

Jews are obligated to be involved in studying Torah simply to study Torah.

As a religious activity, this is unusual.

Most religions have expectations about belief and about doing the right things, but they don't obligate you to study.

Jews, however, study Torah as an independent activity that is not directly connected with belief or action.

In fact, the most studied books in Jewish life, like the Talmud, have little practical use.

So why are people studying the laws of things that happened in remote times—and were rare even then—or things that the Talmud says never happened and never will happen?

We devote time to it because what we are doing is going after knowledge for itself, not as something to be used.

Not everyone has the same level of active curiosity, but study is encouraged and done as an obligation.

The number of classes and lectures available in a Jewish community can't be compared to anything that happens in any other place.

Why does God want us to study?

Theologically, it is a way to commune with Him.

The ability to study for the sake of study is what I call a true human trait in which we are, in a way, higher than angels.

Angels don't seem to have curiosity; they know everything. And animals learn only what they need to live. So the only beings who are curious about anything are people.

This notion was always powerful within Jewish life, and it has pushed some people to high intellectual levels.

Isidor Rabi—who won the Nobel Prize for Physics in 1944—attributed his prize and his great achievements to his parents.

When he came home from school, they never asked him what he learned.

Rather, they wanted to know, "Did you ask a good question today?"

CHAPTER 17

The *Mitzvot*: Understanding God's Commandments

"The mitzvot *may be likened to the vertebrae of the spine. Even if only one is slightly damaged or shifted out of place, it may cause enormous disruption and trouble, but when each functions properly, each as a link in the unity, they constitute a working harmony."*

Whoever grabs hold can reach the other side

God descends on Mount Sinai with great noise and thunder, but what, after all, does He say?

If one holds up these messages to careful scrutiny, one finds them to be at best no more than a few succinct injunctions that were fairly well known and necessary in the ancient world:

Thou shall not steal, thou shall not commit murder, thou shall not commit adultery, and so forth.

Does God have to descend from Heaven just to instruct the members of a fugitive tribe about things they could learn by themselves if they took the trouble?

The point is that what God says is unique and special, not in terms of content but because it is God Himself who says it.

Included are the ethical formulas, "thou shall not do" and "thou shall do" this or that, which are all part of the human structure.

But when the same injunction is part of a Divine communication, it acquires another dimension of power and meaning.

As, for example, in music, the intervals and emphasis are just as important as the notes themselves.

The silence around the sound is what gives it meaning, like the space around a shape.

So that the *mitzvah* may be regarded as no more than an exteriorization of social ritual, a human act, while the Torah, which revealed the *mitzvah,* is what makes this *mitzvah* a vehicle for Divine unity.

Not only because it is what God wants but because He has extended His hand across the abyss of the world, saying, in effect, that whoever grabs hold can reach the other side.

The performance of the *mitzvah* may lie beyond one's understanding

Revelation is not necessarily a phenomenon of thunder and lightning and the sounding of trumpets.

It may be seen as a constellation of forces, an unforeseen combination of things.

God indicates a way that consists of a simple integration of certain elements.

Specific objects, times, and places, and more or less defined actions, words, and thoughts, when combined, serve to produce inestimable effects.

Whether one is aware of these effects or whether one feels any lofty sentiment or satisfaction is irrelevant.

The performance of the *mitzvah* may lie beyond one's understanding, so that one feels a certain strangeness and incompatibility.

It doesn't make any difference. For the *mitzvah* does not rely on thoughts or feelings. Its point of departure is relationships.

The Divine code is not easily given to comprehension, but one can do the *mitzvah* as best one can, in the way one transmits a message in code, trying to avoid mistakes or distortion, clinging faithfully to whatever contact one has with the source.

Carrying out the commandments

The significance of a *mitzvah* lies in its function as a vehicle for God's will.

The hand that distributes charity is, in one way or another, the hand of God, an instrument of His power.

If all the life of a person is devoted to carrying out the commandments, that person may be said to become a vehicle of the *Shekhinah,* the Divine presence.

Every *mitzvah* is a part of a whole

The *mitzvot* may be likened to the vertebrae of the spine.

Even if only one is slightly damaged or shifted out of place, it may cause enormous disruption and trouble, but when each functions properly, each as a link in the unity, they constitute a working harmony.

Every *mitzvah* is a part of a whole.

And I, as a man, merely join them together, as one joins water pipes or electric wire to allow the passage of whatever it is that flows.

I myself do not create the current. I merely make it possible for it to flow, with greater or lesser freedom.

At one end, there is the Infinite light and, at the other, the speck of soul, which is both myself and a spark of the Divine. As it is written in Ecclesiastes 12:2, "Until the silver cord be cut."

This silver cord has been mystically likened to the spine, and every *mitzvah* to a link in it, through which the Divine light flows.

Every *mitzvah* is important

A person who performs a *mitzvah* is in two dimensions of reality: normal existence, in which the *mitzvah* is a fixed act at a very specific point in space and time, and eternity, where time altogether ceases to have any meaning.

There is the story of the rabbi who was jokingly asked by a well-to-do member of the congregation, "Tell me, Rabbi, is it not true that in the prayer of the *Shema* it is written that for someone who transgresses, the rain will not fall and his work will not prosper? Well, look at me; all my life I did not pay attention to the laws of the Torah; I don't keep the *mitzvot* now, and yet I have wealth and honor. How do you explain it?"

And the rabbi answered, "From what you have said, I gather that you were once accustomed to reciting the *Shema* prayer. And you should know that there is nothing great enough to reward you for this single *mitzvah* of reciting the *Shema.* As for your transgressions, that is something else."

Thus every *mitzvah* is a genuine moment of contact with the Eternal, and there can be nothing in life to balance it.

Good and bad deeds do not cancel each other out

Mitzvot and transgressions are neither complementary nor opposite poles, like plus and minus, which cancel each other out.

It is true that there is an ultimate judgment of good and evil in which an individual life is weighed in the balance.

But that judgment examines each separate action by itself.

The good deeds do not influence the badness of the bad deeds, and the bad deeds, no matter how many or how terrible, cannot alter the existence or the value of the humblest good.

There is no common denominator between them.

The importance of intention

Great importance is attached to intention.

There is the story of the *tzaddik* who wanted a special person to blow the shofar at the New Year festival. There were a number of outstanding candidates, and he asked each one what his intention was—why did he wish to blow the shofar?

One after another, they gave very fine answers about their motives and thoughts.

One mentioned the *kavvanot* of Rabbi Isaac Luria.

Another spoke of the intentions of another sage.

Finally, they came to one who said he needed money to feed his children. Upon hearing this, the *tzaddik* said that this man was the right man.

One could never be sure about the sincerity of the others, but this man's intentions came from the very core of his being.

What, then, is *kavvanah* (intention)? It would appear that intensity of will, of truth, is of more value than intellectual content.

The strength and capacity of a *mitzvah* depend on the life force one puts into it

Since the aim of human life on earth is to redeem this world by bringing it up to some level of contact with the Divine, aspiring to higher levels of proper intention is a vital aspect of this process of correction.

If a person has the opportunity to perform a *mitzvah,* either he chooses to do it only with his body, with its circumscribed field of force and of life, or he chooses to harness it to the power of his thought and feeling, giving it a certain orientation and additional potency.

Like any act that one may perform, such as digging with one's hands or digging with a tractor, the action is the same, but its power is different.

So, too, the *mitzvah,* whether it is giving charity or reciting a blessing, is always itself. Its strength and capacity depend on the life force one puts into it, and this is mainly a matter of the heart's intention and the thoughts of the knowledgeable mind.

It is true that intention without the body can have no effect whatsoever. But together with the physical act, it can effect a crucial change in the essence of the world.

The three parts of a *mitzvah*

A *mitzvah* is made up of three parts: the will of the One who commands it, the system or technique of the action, and the person who performs the *mitzvah.*

None of these by itself is enough. Only by someone performing it is a *mitzvah* genuine and holy.

Tefillin lying on a shelf are no more than little boxes and straps. The *tzitzit* are no more than threads. A Torah scroll is holy only when the right person reads from it in the right way.

Only when the circle of Divine will is closed and the circuit of holiness is complete is there a *mitzvah.*

A higher level of functioning

When one studies a halakhah, the way of Torah, about the performance of a ritual, such as the lighting of the Hanukkah candles, and it becomes apparent, through study, that a source of flame that is fed like a bonfire is not a proper Hanukkah candle, one is taking part in the idea behind the ritual as well as performing it.

One is identifying with the Divine will in the matter and not only obeying it.

By becoming involved in the reasons for the action and the correct way of doing it, one is raised to a higher level of functioning, like one who reads the plans for a building under construction and does not merely lay the bricks.

The conservation of spiritual essences

An action does not just vanish into nothingness. Everything is conserved.

The idea is not inconsistent with modern thinking, which admits to the law of the conservation of energy and of matter and recognizes that there is no end to the forms that existence may take.

Not only are there material consequences and residues, but there is also a certain transformation of subtle energies and thought contents.

New forms are assumed, and there is movement into another frame of reference, such as the spiritual.

There is also a law of conservation of spiritual essences.

The spiritual contents of a human action are subject to alteration and can become something very definite, such as a being of the angelic order.

In other words, the spiritual essence of a *mitzvah,* its inner content, constitutes a certain existence that becomes a force seeking its own level and framework of expression.

It has to be retained somehow in the structure of things that are real.

It is not a matter of instruments or means to an end; it is simply that one's actions remain and cling to one's life.

The angels or the demonic creatures I create swarm about me and cry, "Father, you are the one who brought us into existence." I cannot, therefore, cast my life away from myself, out of sight behind my back.

Only the process of repentance can change things and erase some of the past or at least cut the connection with certain actions or states of mind of the past.

All the *mitzvot* together form a symphonic whole

Once a certain rabbi was visited by the Baal Shem Tov, the great leader of the Hasidic movement, on the Day of Atonement, Yom Kippur.

To his astonishment, the Baal Shem Tov kept singing the awesome prayer of repentance, *Al Chet,* literally "For the Sin," in a clearly happy melody.

It was more like a marching tune than a recital of guilt and remorse, reflecting the liveliness of transgression more than the sorrow of contrition.

The rabbi could not help asking the meaning of such impious singing, and he received the reply:

"Anyone who is a genuinely devoted servant of the King will sing whenever he is carrying out the King's orders, whether he comes as a victor in battle or whether he is cleaning out the filth from the homes. Since the King's instructions for this day are to do repentance, to clean out the filth, I sing as I would at any opportunity to do His will."

The performance of any *mitzvah* is a joy, whether it be a likable task or a disagreeable one, a significant act or something relatively trivial.

All the *mitzvot* together form a symphonic whole, a single command, a collective summoning of our response.

Following the Code of Law is not enough

Man is in a ceaseless state of conflict, suspended between the holy and the other side.

He has to know where each is located, and mere adherence to the *Shulkhan Arukh,* the Code of Law, is not enough.

There are many areas and situations that require understanding and spiritual discrimination.

CHAPTER 18

Kabbalah

"Kabbalah is the official theology of the Jewish people. It is the route to gaining a better understanding of the relationship between man and God."

Some books of Jewish history denied the existence of Kabbalah

Kabbalah is the chief repository of the mystical aspect of the tradition, and in Europe, it was taken firmly in hand.

Only mature students were permitted to study it, and carefully preserved texts were left to gather dust and sink into oblivion.

In later years, mostly in the nineteenth century, there was another, newer element that helped suppress the mystical lore.

Within the strong rationalistic tendency of the age, many influential people, including the authors of some of the most important books of Jewish history, were fiercely antagonistic to any mystical approach and tried to disparage it and even deny its existence.

The apologetic mode of the time demanded hiding these "shameful" parts of Judaism and trying to forget them entirely.

The result has been a general misunderstanding of the role of Kabbalah and of the mystical experience altogether in Judaism.

Hasidism is a form of applied Kabbalah

It is a basic Kabbalistic concept that the human soul is, in a manner of speaking, a spark of Divine revelation in the world and that each human being is a microcosm of the entire universe.

Hasidism shows how the rarefied teachings of Kabbalah, which speak to the macro-universe, can be adapted into a structure with ethical and practical meaning for our individual lives.

In this way, Hasidism is a form of applied Kabbalah.

Just as the Revealed Law frames the behavior of our bodies, the internalization of Kabbalistic notions of the Hidden Law can attune us to our soul, educating it to connect with the Divine. In this model, the power of Kabbalah is harnessed not to serve our own desires but to align them with the wishes of the Almighty.

One of the most important Hasidic books is called *Zohar Chai*, "The Living *Zohar.*"

That is what Hasidism does: it gives the Kabbalah life by translating it into something meaningful in one's relationships with others and, most important, something that can quell the strife within one's own soul and calm the struggle of one's inner being.

The official theology of the Jewish people

One must be cautioned that when speaking about Kabbalah, it does not refer to the numerous imitations being sold nowadays in the form of little booklets, red strings, and healing waters.

All of these approaches take the name of Kabbalah in vain, for the utmost secrets of the world and the promise of eternal life, protective angels, and supreme devotion cannot be purchased for five cents apiece.

This type of commercialized mysticism is surely more propagated today than authentic Kabbalah and has the dangerous ability to deceive the masses into believing that they have discovered the essence of Kabbalah.

Kabbalah is—or at least has been for the last five hundred years—the official theology of the Jewish people.

It is the route to gaining a better understanding of the relationship between man and God.

Kabbalah and Talmud: different forms of the same thing

Customarily, we speak of the different ways of dealing with Torah, from the explicit to the implicit, from *peshat* (literal meaning), to *remez* (hint), to *derash* (exegesis), to *sod* (secret or esoteric truth).

All these simply address the same words of Scripture in four different languages, all of which have the same meaning.

One of the methods of study is to gain an understanding of the way these languages change from one form of expression to another, how they change from saying something in poetic terms to those of a story, a commandment, and a Kabbalistic idea.

Consequently, the common view about mysticism and Kabbalah being a different world from the Talmud is a misconception of the organic unity of the whole.

The Kabbalah and the Talmud are different forms of expression, each following its own point of departure.

The greatest of the Jewish authorities were immersed in the world of Kabbalah

The *Shulkhan Arukh,* the great work that has become the fundamental legal, halakhic text for all of Jewry, was written by Rabbi Joseph Karo, a sage whose authority rested not only on his very broad learning but also on his many-sidedness and mystic insight.

He wrote other books of halakhic procedure and law and exegeses on Torah and the like, and in addition he wrote a treatise called *Maggid M'esharim*, which was a Kabbalistic work and showed him to be a man who had mystical experiences and visions.

Those of his generation who heard about his revelations were inclined to say that it was the voice of the Mishnah speaking from his mouth.

To this day, the inspired orders of prayers we follow on the all-night *Tikkun Leil Shavuot* of Shavuot are those of Rabbi Joseph Karo.

And one of his closest disciples wrote the famous Shabbat song *Lechah Dodi,* now accepted in all circles of Jewish worship, which is obviously a Kabbalistic poem.

So we see that the greatest of the halakhic legal authorities were very much immersed in the mystical world of Kabbalah.

Kabbalah needs more than a smattering of knowledge

Personally, I am not for this new Kabbalah trend. I think it is cheap and I think it presents a danger.

Not that people are learning too much Kabbalah but that they are focusing only on the mystery and secret and magic and don't address how people should change or become more Jewish.

Kabbalah is not a gimmick. It is something holy and serious, and it needs much more than a smattering of knowledge.

Imagine taking a six-week course in neurosurgery and hanging up a shingle. It is not only fraudulent but dangerous.

We study the secret lore but don't see angels

As some Hasidim used to say, "We study the secret lore, learn about the existence of other worlds, angels, seraphs, and Heavenly beings.

But I don't see any angels or Heavenly beings, and I don't believe that anyone who studies more is able to see more."

Nevertheless, the difference between the one who studies and the one who does not study is that in the future, when these things are made manifest, the one who studies will be able to recognize them better, to relate them to what he has learned.

PART V

The Trials of Life

"The good is hidden, and several levels have to be excavated in order to get to it."

CHAPTER 19

Struggles, Battles, and Trials

"To fall is not a sign of failure but rather an indication that one is making progress."

Climbing from level to level

There is a story of the sage who did not want to go to the synagogue on Yom Kippur, saying, "Last year, I claimed to be penitent and to return to God, but since this has proved to be false, I do not desire to repeat it."

The others consoled him by telling him to say, "Lord God, this time I speak truly, with all the sincerity of my heart."

A person can promise something with all his heart, and if it turns out that he is unable to carry it out, it only means that the promise lacks the truth of eternity.

It does not repudiate the truth of the present, this moment of life, and this level of one's inner being.

There is a general law to the effect that the lower degree of a higher level is a little higher than the highest degree of a lower level.

And this is true of all the stages and degrees of being.

All that was previously true may become untrue as a person rises. What was yesterday my Heaven has to become my earth today.

And tomorrow there will be higher Heavens and truths that are today beyond my grasp.

Everyone experiences setbacks

Ideal people who know no backsliding have never existed except as figments of the imagination and of literary invention.

No Jew, even the greatest leader, saint, or prophet, has ever been free of religious problems, failings, heartaches, and doubts.

It is an established principle: everyone who takes the religious life seriously and who is thus ever striving onward experiences setbacks along the way.

It is not merely that "there is no one so righteous that he does only good and never sins," but more than this:

Temptation, doubt, pain, and transgression are the inevitable lot of those who would ascend higher.

All seekers are not on the same level, and their failings are thus not equally grave.

A great person who falls back may still be on a much higher plane than others. In both the material and the spiritual realms, "the righteous man may fall down seven times and yet arise."

Though he falls again and again, he continues to grope his way upward.

This is the strength of the righteous: their ability to endure crisis, to bounce back, and to turn failure into a source of strength.

To fall is a sign that one is making progress

The falling and the rising and the falling again are indications of an unending conflict within.

This is important because sometimes a person may feel that his failure or decline is a sign of something essentially wrong.

To fall is not a sign of failure but rather an indication that one is making progress, that something essential is alive within one, something that, if it is lacking, makes progress impossible and invites the Angel of Death.

In the Jewish way of life, the challenge is constant

It has been said that it is difficult to be a Jew because one cannot simply go to the synagogue and pray and then go about one's affairs with a purified mind and soul.

The whole crux of Jewish life lies in what takes place during the busy hours of one's affairs as well as in the hours of prayer.

One cannot reside in two worlds at once.

There cannot be any pretense of having done one's spiritual duty at some other time or place.

In the Jewish way of life, the challenge is constant.

The power of repentance

The greater the person, the greater his potential for evil. As our sages note, "When a person is greater than another, his evil inclination is greater as well" (*Sukkah* 52a).

The fact that a person has a great evil inclination indicates that he can become a great and religious person.

The Hasidic rebbe Rabbi Levi Yitzchak of Berditchev once inspired a man to repent by telling him, "I envy you. When a person repents in a spirit of love, his willful misdeeds are accounted as merits. How great you can become when you repent!"

A true penitent stands on a higher level

A person who has sinned for many years feels an immense vacuum in that part of his life.

Although he strives desperately to fill it, there seems to be an emptiness that nothing can satisfy, and his past evildoing, even if thoroughly repented, becomes part of the structure of his soul.

This is why it is said that a true penitent, with his extra power of recollected sin, stands on a higher level than a saint who has never sinned at all.

The nature of the transformation is more like a chemical change, a change of essence rather than a change of form or place.

Everything that was true of a person is transmuted into a different substance.

The King of Kings is watching our every move

The *Shulkhan Arukh*, the Code of Jewish Law, instructs the reader to wake in the morning with the thought that the King of Kings, the Lord Himself, in all His greatness and glory, is standing over him and watching his every move, so that he should jump out of bed and begin to serve the Lord as best he can.

However, as we know, even the wisest of men find this difficult.

Straightening out the distortions

Rabbi Nachman of Bratslav once said that there is a certain distortion in the world. Before one can relate to any reality beyond it, one has to straighten the distortion out.

One has to effect a certain series of transformations in order to get some semblance of the Truth. Once one has reached such a valid picture of the Truth, one can function in the world in an effective manner.

This is what is known as the "secret of the fathers," which is the *merkavah*, the Chariot, the secret of those who possess the Truth.

Prayer is a time of battle between mighty forces

Prayer is more than reciting the words of the prayer book, which in itself requires no great struggle.

Prayer is a time of battle between mighty forces, as the soul wrestles with all of the opposing forces surrounding it.

This is a spiritual and physical effort in which one concentrates thought and attention, oblivious to everything outside.

The combination of such unswerving focus with the effort to arrive at a higher level of union with the Divine and a spiritual elevation demands what *Tanya* calls "a strenuous war."

Prayer is a trial against oneself

The Hebrew word *tefillah,* prayer, shares the same root as *naftolin,* struggle.

Prayer is a wrestling of man with the angel, the struggle of man with the Holy One, blessed be He.

Tefillah is also connected with *plilim,* jurisprudence.

Prayer is a trial in which man is brought to court against himself, in which he judges his world and pleads his case with his Maker.

The necessity of instability

When a person passes from one level to another, there is an increased danger of falling. He is no longer secure in the previous level and can easily fall before he gains a hold in the next level.

This is true for every change in condition or of level of existence.

For instance, when entering the water to swim, there is a moment when one has to lose balance, disconnect from the secure contact with the ground, and be neither walking nor floating.

Transition thus always involves imbalance and danger.

If someone who is learning some skill, either manual or intellectual, is put into a situation where there is a real difference of approach to the subject, it seems fairly necessary to advise the person to forget all that he had learned previously because it would only serve to confuse him.

He cannot progress to a higher level of performance without forgetting, letting go of what he already knows.

So that those people, for example, who are intrinsically unable to forget are also those who find it hard to progress.

The passage from one level to another demands a sort of leap, an abandoning of all that was solid ground.

It is a basic feature of human progress, resting on the principle that the interval between points or fields comprises a mode of nothingness, and one cannot proceed from one point to another without losing one's previous balance, even if only for the briefest moment.

Tying the broken cord

There is a phrase in the book of Ecclesiastes: "Or ever the silver cord be loosed" (12:6).

This cord has been likened to an umbilical cord binding man to God, a cord made up of numerous strands, the 613 commandments of the religious life.

Whenever a man transgresses, he cuts one of the strands and, strand by strand, severs himself from God.

Man is given a certain amount of time to try to repair the severed thread, to tie it together by repentance and right action.

And it is said that a strand so tied together is stronger than one that has never been torn.

Just as a broken bone forms a hard knob when it knits together, making it stronger than before, this is ultimately the proof of the repentant sinner: he is more steady and powerful than before.

CHAPTER 20

Suffering

"Suffering is a trial. . . . For suffering can lead to many things. Some rise; others fall. Suffering is the test. Can a person receive it without sliding into hatred? Can he grow from experiencing it?"

Bless God for the evil as well as the good

The story is told about two Torah scholars who asked the great Maggid of Mezritch about the Talmudic dictum that "a person must bless God for the evil just as he blesses Him for the good" (*Berachot* 60b).

The Maggid sent them to his student, Rabbi Zusha of Anipoli.

Throughout his life, Rabbi Zusha lived in dire poverty.

But when these two men came to him with their question, Rabbi Zusha replied, "I don't understand why the rebbe sent you to me. I've never had a bad moment in my life."

In other words, he who reaches a certain level does not come to grips with the problems of evil.

It does not even touch him.

By his very existence, he simply transforms all darkness to light.

Thanking God for suffering is easier said than done

On thanking God for the evil as well as for the good that happens, it is known to be far more difficult in the doing than in the saying.

There is the story of Rabbi Meizlish of Krakow and Warsaw, who was a rich merchant before he became a rabbi.

He was famous for his erudition, and he used to teach brilliant pupils at the yeshiva.

During this time he continued in business, sending timber along the river to Germany to be sold there at a profit.

The news came that the timber rafts were wrecked in a storm, and the rabbi's whole fortune was lost in one day.

They did not know how to tell the rabbi and chose one of his favorite pupils to do so.

The young man selected a passage in the Talmud and came to the rabbi with his question: "It says here that one has to thank God with blessings for the evil that befalls one as well as for the good. How can this be done?"

The rabbi explained the matter in terms of its hidden meaning as well as in straightforward theology.

To this the pupil replied, "I am not sure I understand. If my rabbi were to learn that all his timber rafts were wrecked on the river, would he dance for joy?"

The rabbi said, "Yes, of course."

"Well, then," said the pupil, "you can dance. All the rafts are lost!"

Upon hearing this, the rabbi fainted.

When he came to, he said, "Now I must confess that I no longer understand this Talmud passage."

Everything is for the best

To be sure, everything is good, in the sense that it comes from God.

On the other hand, there can be no denying that suffering exists and that the cause of suffering is something that may be called evil.

In this case, the good is hidden, and several levels have to be excavated in order to get to it.

On the simplest level, one can sometimes see it quite directly. My cow broke a leg, and I found a treasure at that spot.

Or there is the story of Rabbi Akiva, who, traveling, could not get lodging at the inn.

He had, however, a candle to read by, a donkey to take him to the forest where he could sleep, and a rooster to wake him in the morning.

So he was pleased and said, "This, too, is for the best."

Then a lion came and killed his donkey. A cat devoured his rooster. And the wind snuffed out his candle.

"This, too, is for the best," he said, and he curled up in a tree and slept soundly.

In the morning, he learned that a band of wild robbers had come to the inn, looted it, and taken captive all who were there.

Had his donkey neighed or his cock crowed, or had the robbers seen his candle, he, too, would have been plundered. So he was able to say again with conviction, "This, too, is for the best."

Suffering is a test

Consider the simple situation of a person in a certain distress, whether of a greater or a lesser degree—a lack of money or illness or a calamity of tragic proportions or despondency.

The distress is genuine enough.

There is no point in claiming that one should be glad about it or that one should not do everything possible to eliminate it.

The usual way of relating to distress is to experience a certain drop of spirit, a sadness, or bitterness, which can be interpreted as stemming from an attitude that one does not deserve the pain and sorrow, that one has somehow been unfairly or wrongly treated.

This can be remedied by seeing the suffering not as punishment for some wrongdoing that one may or may not have done but as a sort of reward, which is not immediately apparent as such.

It takes a while to distinguish it.

Another part of the problem lies in the nature of whatever causes distress. What if it gets worse? What if no good comes of it?

Suffering is a trial. For suffering can lead to many things.

Some rise; others fall. Suffering is the test.

Can a person receive it without sliding into hatred?

Can he grow from experiencing it?

It is a privilege to weep before Him

The general mood of the biblical book of Lamentations is interwoven not only with faith in God and in the rightness of His judgment but also with a deep and even intimate bond between the mourner and God.

Not only is the Lord always present, but it is possible, and even a privilege, to weep before Him.

The relation to God with all the heartache and suffering is not a relation to the "Judge of the whole earth" or to "King of the world" but to the "Merciful Father."

The blows that He distributes are not the blows of wickedness.

The sufferings that he causes have a good reason.

But the fact that the judgment is just does not eliminate the pain.

The fact that the son receives his suffering without striking back does not diminish the suffering.

Yet the son knows that he is allowed to cry.

He knows that he can put his head in the father's lap, the same father who lashed out at him, and that he can tell him how much he is suffering.

As described in the many dirges, poems, and prayers of the sages, God Himself weeps over the destruction of the Temple.

He Himself suffers and feels the agony of those who are stricken. Indeed, many of these are more specific delineations of the mood of the book of Lamentations.

Much more than the mourner is addressing his countrymen, those who are with him and those who will remember these events in the future, he is really addressing God Himself.

It is not a petition or even a protest. It is rather an outpouring of the heart, a weeping on the part of one who knows that the chastising father is suffering his pain along with him.

God needs your particular pains

A parable relates the story of a man of the people who came to one of the *tzaddikim,* crying bitterly, "I have such awful pains, headaches, and worries. I can neither pray nor study. What will be the end of me?"

The *tzaddik* answered, "You are greatly mistaken. You think that God needs your prayers and your studies? If He had any such need, He would place a few thousand angels to pray and study for Him. God needs your particular pains and your headache and your worries. For this He cannot get angelic or human help. Only you can supply it."

It is often necessary to pass through some crisis or tragic experience

Sometimes there is a real need for a contrite heart. The greatest hindrance to spiritual awakening is smugness, a dullness of the heart and mind.

All the books and all the messages of spiritual love will not avail. In fact, complacency is a more serious obstacle than depression or stupidity.

To overcome it, to smash through the barrier of "fatness" of the soul, it is often necessary to pass through some sort of crisis or tragic experience. And this is often brought about by Heavenly intervention, against one's own wishes and designs.

It is a disquieting fact that it is more difficult to gain knowledge of the Divine through ordinary, positive living than through negative or tragic experience.

The negative seems to have much more power to break down one's resistance; the positive tends to reinforce one's smugness.

The only world in which Creation makes sense

There are certain mysteries that simply cannot be answered. One of these is the question that asks about the purpose of Creation.

As one Hasidic rebbe said with respect to this very question, there is language in the Midrash to the effect that the Almighty had a *taivah,* a desire, and if you have a desire, you don't ask why.

The language of the Midrash is very suggestive at this point because a *taivah* is something we can't explain. Answering a question about the "why" of Creation can be proved, philosophically, to be impossible. You get to a point where you are asking questions that are unanswerable, not because you lack knowledge but because they are unanswerable by definition.

But perhaps we can say this much:

When you speak about the world from this point of view, it is, so to speak, a tour de force, an experiment in existence, an experiment of what I might call "conquering the utmost case."

In a way, existence in any other world is not "proof." Proof in the utmost case occurs only when you can do things under the worst of circumstances.

If I want to test a new car, the way that I test it is not on the smoothest of roads, under the best conditions.

To have a real road test to prove that a car really works, I have to put it under the worst conditions in which there is yet hope.

I cannot test it by driving it off a cliff, but I can test it on the roughest terrain where I must come to the edge of a cliff and have to stop.

How is a new airplane tested? They put it under nearly impossible conditions, which the plane must withstand. Otherwise the whole experiment doesn't prove anything.

The same with Creation.

Creation would have been pointless unless it was a Creation under precisely these difficult circumstances.

Theologically speaking, the worst possible world in which there is yet hope is the only world in which Creation makes sense.

The more pure a man is, the more he is tempted

It is said that the Divine seems to go out of His way to provoke scholars and saints.

One who is superior to his fellows has to suffer more from the provocations of the evil impulse.

The more pure and more holy the man is, the more he is prey to the parasitic forces of evil.

Also, the self-punishment of the righteous is proportionately severe.

The ironic thing is that, in itself, the evil impulse is quite impotent.

It cannot really do much harm, being nothing more than a negation, a zero, devoid of real being of its own.

The wholeness of a broken heart

Just as a ladder cannot be useful unless it has something to lean against, so, too, is there nothing more whole than a broken heart.

Even though, to be sure, God prefers vessels that are without blemishes or cracks, and it is written in the *Zohar* that the *Shekhinah* does not lodge itself anywhere except in a whole vessel.

Nevertheless, this does not include a broken heart.

As Rabbi Schneur Zalman of Liadi mentions, if one does not have a broken and contrite heart, one cannot be said to have a heart at all.

Understanding the difference between pain and sadness

Suffering by itself is not a matter of being mistreated by life.

It is something given that has to be received, sometimes as a gift.

Pain and sadness are two very different qualities.

Sadness is a state of mind in which a person perceives himself as rather justified and decent, while God is rather unfair.

One should avoid falling into anxiety and sadness.

A strategy to banish sadness

Sadness can be a vehicle for attaining something else, a bitter remedy for a worse ailment.

On the other hand, life furnishes enough genuine reasons for being downcast.

In order to prevent sadness from being a dominant factor in life, we appoint special times for it, such as fast days or days of potential prayer, and banish it from the rest of our lives.

The worst possible world where there is still hope

The evil in our world is the very lowest state of being.

The world we live in is the lowest of the worlds, and it is the only world in which not only evil can exist but even willful evil, rebelliously and freely chosen.

It is not the bacteria of cholera that are evil.

It is man who makes it so.

The destructive bacteria are part of an independent system that can be one thing or another, but they are ultimately performing the Divine Will.

This is not the same as what the philosopher Leibniz said, that this world of ours is the best of all possible worlds.

It is more like what Voltaire maintained, that it is the depth of corruption.

What is being added is that our world is the worst of all worlds in which correction (*tikkun*) is still possible.

Our world is still balanced, albeit rather precariously, on the edge of the abyss of evil, but it can still rise up and extricate itself.

Were it only a little worse, it would be a world without hope of redemption.

Were a world worse than ours to exist, it would no longer be a world—it would be Hell.

From this, we recognize that the final verdict is optimistic, that although this dark and evil world may not be so wonderful, there is still hope for it.

In the struggle of existence, one discovers the harmony

For all men, the world is a public domain full of shells and temptations and blind forces of nature.

A person living in the world feels as though he were located on the other side of the mountains of darkness, in an incoherent multiplicity of systems, rather than in a single stable universe.

There is no purpose or direction.

The public domain seems to be a rather wild, amoral, and chaotic place.

It is in this public domain, with its mountains of separation, dividing man from God, that one can be transformed into a private domain of light and unity.

The very struggle for existence is a gradual learning process in which one discovers the singleness and the harmony behind the multiplicity and the disorder.

The joys of the next world

There is no way of comparing the pleasures of this world—for all their sweetness, intensity, and variety—with the pleasure of the next world.

We have no common denominator.

Just as we cannot compare a color, such as blue, with a number.

We can have more blueness or less, a larger number or a smaller one; we cannot compare them.

All we can say about the joys of the next world is that they are so superior to the joys of this world that it is worth going through the torments of Hell in order to attain them.

CHAPTER 21

Evil

"The greatness of man stems from the struggle between good and evil."

Understanding evil

Evil is not the same as what many would classify as unmitigated wickedness.

As in most things, a certain education of the moral sense allows one to see things differently.

In matters of taste, the bitterness of certain beverages, like beer, has to be cultivated in order to be enjoyed, in contrast to the obvious sweetness of sugary things, which is almost always enjoyed.

Or consider the whole gamut of sophisticated taste in art, as well as in culinary matters.

The development of "good taste" requires time.

So, too, it is easy to bless that which is universally good. It is difficult to comprehend the true nature of suffering and, even more so, to "enjoy it."

The truth of things is hidden.

The true good is on a higher level of reality, making it less available to our understanding.

Evil is a parasite

Evil is a perversion. It is the exploitative misuse of holiness.

This creates an illusion, a false world that misuses the power of life and truth of holiness to support its existence.

Complete falsehood is an abstract concept.

To exist, a falsehood must possess a grain of truth, not only to be persuasive but also so that one will be able to express it.

It is a shadow that cannot exist without the light that surrounds it. The existence of evil is not its own, not intrinsic, but drawn from holiness.

According to one theory about the structure of microscopic organisms, a virus is basically no more than a genetic code.

This virus attaches itself to an existing biological structure and perverts it in keeping with its code.

In essence, the existence of the virus is perversion.

In itself, it cannot create life.

It possesses no more than the ability to parasitically attach itself and create forms within others.

With that power it lives, and with that power it perverts its world in order to create a world of illusion.

This virus does not wage war against the body.

It does not have specific programs and intentions with regard to the body.

It simply grows and develops, and as it does so, it increasingly perverts and destroys the organism to which it is attached.

Evil, too, is a parasite. If it could be isolated and separated from holiness, it would cease to live and exist.

What it has is not its own, and what is its own is nothing.

Evil must be fought

In our world, which is so full of information of every possible kind, especially about lesser and inferior things, which is what sells newspapers and brings high ratings to TV shows, it should have been natural for people to be well aware of the existence of evil.

Nevertheless, it seems, oddly enough, that people still do not really know that evil, as a force with a power of its own, actually exists.

In terms of worldview, it seems that the Victorian way of thinking still very much shapes people's consciousness.

Everyone surely knows that here and there, there are distorted and wicked human beings.

But they are seen as oddities that are not part of real life.

There really is evil in the world.

It has its own ideology and organizations. It exists not just somewhere far away but here, so very close to everyone's daily life.

This ideology is not necessarily connected to people of a particular religion, color, race, or creed.

It belongs to those who allow evil to control them to such an extent that human life has lost all value in their eyes.

Their plan—or rather, that of their leaders—crushes and kills men and women, old and young, guilty and innocent alike.

Although people are hurt by the activities of this evil, there still exists a desire to find some justification for it.

People try to explain evil away, especially when it relates to others.

They speak about national uprising, poverty, and illiteracy, about unbridled incitement.

No doubt, all these things do exist.

They do not by any means, however, justify evil or even furnish a valid explanation for it.

This sort of evil is not spontaneous.

Rather, it is planned and controlled by cold-blooded people who have no compunctions about killing their victims as well as their messengers.

These leaders of evil do not operate alone.

They are assisted by the innocent, the indifferent, and the foolish.

The innocents are those who can find or even invent justifications and explanations for everything.

The indifferent are those who are not moved by disasters that happen to other people in other lands.

The foolish are those who think they have a safe way of escaping disaster.

We must see reality as it is: there are evil, wickedness, and cruelty in this world.

We can and must persecute them down to their most primary sources.

It is possible to fight and, through an extended, concentrated effort, also to eradicate them.

In any case, we must remember that there are things in this world that decent human beings must fight against and annihilate.

The struggle with the evil inclination

It makes no difference whether the struggle with the evil inclination is over something great or something small, whether a person struggles to withstand sinning or struggles to use one's time wisely.

The battle, in either case, is of equal intensity and importance.

For example, a person who has learned Torah for nine or ten hours may feel unable to continue.

At that moment, the effort to go on is a battle no less demanding than the war against the evil inclination's most fiery desires.

In the final analysis, there is no qualitative difference between a person who sins because he gave in to the distractions of the street and a scholar who does not increase his study schedule or pray with *kavvanah*.

Neither is prepared to struggle, and neither steps beyond his limitations.

After one has defeated the evil impulse, it ceases to have any meaning

The greatness of man stems from the struggle between good and evil.

This is why God has to build the anomaly of evil, making it possible for it to exist and flourish and then, when it has performed its function, making it null and void.

After one has defeated the evil impulse, it ceases to have any meaning.

The ceaseless war that man wages can be interpreted as a challenge for him to do all that he can while God is working against him at the other end. As soon a man proves that he is able to stand the test, it all collapses and has no more significance.

And then something else starts up all over again.

No two people are alike in their susceptibility to temptation

No two people are alike.

This includes their susceptibility to temptation.

Some people are left cold by stimuli that others find impossible to resist: sexuality, money, and so forth.

The fact that some people are by nature not easily aroused in one or more areas should not make them feel superior.

Like a blind person who would be foolish to congratulate himself on not being tempted by his eyes, a dispassionate person cannot view his lack of passion as a sign of superiority.

Our thoughts give birth to demons

We ourselves create demons in our lives, not in the form of a *dybbuk* who enters into us and causes trouble and consternation, but rather in the form of creatures to which our thoughts give birth.

For every human being continually brings into existence a long line of spiritual offspring.

Transforming evil into good

The righteous person, the *tzaddik,* transforms the evil to good within himself, as well as within the context of the world.

The *tzaddik* does not feel suffering in the same way as other men.

He does not recognize it as something special to be feared and avoided.

It is, for him, like all else in life, a fact of existence.

One eats, one sleeps, one acts, one suffers.

Everything is translated into good.

Developing the capacity to bless evil as well as good

There is a difference between theoretically knowing that God is always present and knowing it when one is crushed.

To be sure, there are many saints, and even ordinary men, who are able to bless the evil as well as the good, not only to receive it without complaint but also to accept it with joy.

The capacity to do so is a function of deeper comprehension as well as of faith or certainty in the wisdom of the hidden workings of God.

Hence we understand the meaning of the verse "Happy is the man whom Thou, O God, chasteneth" (Psalms 94:12).

PART VI

Guidance

"A good teacher is one who helps his student learn how *to learn and who teaches him to become a* mensch. *Turning a student into a* mensch *is the greatest possible achievement of any teacher."*

CHAPTER 22

Learning and Teaching

"When one is studying the Torah, one is in direct communion with God. One is not just reading or studying or even seeking inspiration. In Judaism, God and man are talking together."

Freeing the mind of worry

Preparation creates a momentum for prayer.

One must have the proper mind-set, an internal space free of worry, fear, and disturbance.

One method used by some is to make one's mundane reality a springboard to holiness by telling a joke or a story, for example.

Sometimes such a catalyst creates a quiet moment and displaces a person's worries more effectively than reproof could.

The Talmud (*Ta'anit* 22a) tells us that when Elijah the prophet was asked who had earned a place in the world to come, he pointed out a few simple men.

Elijah explained that they had spent their time cheering up sad people.

Such individuals deserve the world to come because they make it possible for others to transcend this world.

The Talmud (*Pesachim* 117a) also tells us that before Rabbah began teaching, he would make his students laugh and so free their minds of worry.

One must investigate each matter specifically

The question is asked whether it is permissible to make judgments.

And the answer is that one does have to judge things all the time.

It is forbidden to accept things en bloc without investigating deeply into each matter specifically.

Every person and situation has to be examined in the context of a surrounding reality.

There is always more than one viewpoint

A *tzaddik* has his limitations precisely because he chooses. And every choice is a possible error.

Even the *tzaddik* can make the wrong choice or err in his judgment.

What is worse, no matter what he does, he may somehow be wrong in terms of absolute ethics or of relative human needs.

For example, there is a commentary on the sin of anger for which Moses paid such a dear penalty.

It is said that he really chose to strike the rock in anger because otherwise the people of Israel would have been put to unbearable shame if a dumb rock would obey the command of God without being compelled to do so.

Nevertheless, beating the rock was a sinful expression of anger, even if to this day an enormous positive response is aroused by the image of Moses striking the rock and making water gush forth.

What on one hand is sin and error can from another viewpoint be good and necessary.

One may forget what was known, but the impression cannot be effaced

Every day, we learn something new and absorb additional information and knowledge.

But it is not as simple as adding something to a storehouse.

It is a complex process of integration.

Knowledge influences the knower. The knower changes with what he learns.

One may also forget what was known, but the impression made by the knowledge cannot be effaced.

One can forget everything that one has learned, but one cannot wipe out the effect it had on the personality.

Which, incidentally, explains why it is forbidden to put to shame a scholar who has lost his ability to remember.

It is assumed that what he once knew remains as a subtle, ineradicable influence.

It may be sufficient for each person to know as much as he can absorb

No one can be said to reach the wisdom of God.

At best, one attains an understanding of a portion of His Torah—concerning an ox that gores a cow, that the *tzitzit* should have four threads, and so forth.

The ancient Egyptians, although they never developed Euclidean geometry, were aware that the square of the sides of a right triangle were always proportional according to a fixed formula.

They were able to lay out their buildings without any difficulty. They did not have to know more for their purposes.

Perhaps it was enough to have a guiding formula in any given situation.

So, too, in terms of wisdom, it may be sufficient for each person to know as much as he can absorb—the level of one's knowledge is a secondary matter.

The sin of an uneducated person is considered unintentional

If an uneducated person purposely neglects to perform a *mitzvah* or commits a sin, his sin is considered unintentional because it lacks the basic element of complete willfulness, including rebellion, denial of a supreme Master, and a conscious turning away from God's will.

This person does not truly understand the meaning of holiness, and he views God and His *mitzvot* as unclear concepts.

He is considered to be acting unwittingly, like a child who breaks an expensive item whose value he cannot appreciate.

Even when such a person acts knowingly, his knowledge does not extend to a full understanding.

To be willful, a person must be aware.

When his consciousness is on a low level, when he does not adequately understand the meaning of sin and *mitzvot,* he cannot be judged on the same scale as someone who does know and comprehend.

The degree of guilt is proportional to one's level of knowledge

The superiority of the scholar and his knowledge of Torah make it all the more urgent for him to be aware of the Divine presence at all times.

His life, as a whole, is an attempt to approach God, so that even the smallest transgression may be more than he can bear, and his guilt is greater.

How vastly different is this case from the person who is free to roam the streets of the world unencumbered by Torah, where everything is allowed.

When one demands that such a free person must exercise control over his thoughts and actions, to fear God and respect the Divine glory, one is asking far more of him than of the righteous.

He has to struggle much harder against himself and against all the habitual ways of his being.

The degree of guilt varies from one person to another, and the atonement required of each, even for the same sin, is proportional to one's level of knowledge and awareness.

The guilt of one who knows Torah and who has ascended to spiritual heights is far greater than that of the one who is ignorant.

I'm interested in almost everything

My first hobby is the Talmud because by profession I am, or I have to describe myself as, a defrocked mathematician. I began as a teacher of mathematics and physics.

I was caught by the Talmud, and I really did not want to be a Talmudist.

I wanted to deal with it as a hobby, but the hobby grew.

I'm still in love with that hobby of mine.

At the same time, I'm interested in almost everything—from detective stories to science fiction to mathematics to animals.

I am also interested in people—sometimes I even like them.

I am interested in good literature, even though I do not read enough of it.

I prefer children's stories to most earnest literature.

I am interested in science for many reasons, and sometimes in politics.

Sometimes I'm also interested in football, if I have time to watch it; if not, I at least read about it in the newspapers.

So I'm interested in what people are interested in, and not because I have some reason, but because I am curious.

I am still trying to learn, and almost everything fascinates me.

So as long as there is something to learn, I like to learn more and to know more about everything.

A true leader can be understood by everyone

Solomon Maimon, a philosopher and writer, was a guest at the table of the Maggid of Mezritch, where, as he relates, the Maggid called each of the company by name and place of origin, apparently without having been told beforehand, and then asked each one to quote a passage from the Torah, whatever came into his head first.

Afterward, the Maggid thought for a moment and delivered a sermon combining all of the disconnected passages quoted by the guests.

He did so with great ease and coherence.

More astonishing was that each of his listeners was convinced that the Maggid was talking to him, and only to him, in connection with what he himself had spontaneously quoted and that it was, in some intimate way, profoundly related to his life.

The study of science

The possibility exists that profane knowledge is something that can help Torah study, like the Rambam's investigations into astronomy.

The story was told of a teacher and pupil who were walking along a path and saw a worm.

The teacher said he was surprised at the small-mindedness of the writer, who maintained that only the sky reflected the glory of God.

After all, a worm also reflects God's glory and, perhaps, showed the wonder of evolution in an even more subtle fashion.

The study of science and other nonsacred knowledge can be a means of approaching God and realizing the awe and love of God in such a convincing manner that it could only enhance the study of Torah.

Adding the instruments of logic and examination can only sharpen the ability to study.

If profane knowledge is indulged in for this purpose, it is like eating for the sake of Heaven: it becomes transformed into holiness.

I have always been suspicious of artificial means—such as mantras or drugs

I have always been very suspicious of resorting to artificial means—it doesn't really matter whether it is a mantra or a drug.

Do you know the book by Aldous Huxley about the gates of Heaven and Hell?

One of his basic points, which I think was a mistake, was that he thought that somehow he had found the key to another realm.

That was the basic notion, and he wrote very beautifully about it.

Now, as more and more people who tried it found out, you don't get a gateway to Heaven.

You get, at most, a gateway into another chamber within yourself.

We may have wonderful experiences, and we clearly have within us more than we know, more than the eye catches, but we are trying to pass over and through the self to the Other.

Now I may find out lots of beautiful things or horrible things within my microcosms, and there may be ways and means and exercises to get there, but the real problem is that this is still my own realm, and what I really want is to go to the Other Side.

There are, I think, somewhere in the United States, a few miles of receiving antennas that are meant specifically to receive calls from outer space.

Just imagine that you receive such a message.

You are overjoyed. You hear a voice, and it's coming from a very small transmitter on the other side of the earth.

It's a wonderful discovery, but that wasn't what you are searching for.

You were searching for something from the other side of nowhere. You didn't want to find something within your realm.

There are three things that are connected—the Jews with the Torah and the Torah with God

The Torah was never considered merely knowledge, as that which one learns with the mind and in which one becomes an expert.

As Hillel Zeitlin, said, "In many religions, there is the notion of a book or doctrine that comes from Heaven, but we Jews believe that the Torah itself is Heaven."

When one is studying the Torah, one is in direct communion with God. One is not just reading or studying or even seeking inspiration.

In Judaism, God and man are talking together.

As it is written in the *Zohar,* there are three things that are connected—the Jews with the Torah and the Torah with God.

We do not delve into the Torah just to know something in our past or to learn how to behave.

To be engaged with Torah is not just the fulfillment of a commandment, a *mitzvah.*

It is in itself being as close to the Almighty as we will ever be.

A good teacher

A good teacher is one who helps his student to learn *how* to learn and who teaches him to become a *mensch.*

Turning a student into a *mensch* is the greatest possible achievement of any teacher.

Whoever does that does something God-like, a real *imitatio Dei:* creating a human being.

When a teacher is a fake, the students know it right away

Character education is not done through direct statements, such as "be nice" or "be honest."

Children are very clever. They also observe their teachers from every possible angle.

It is therefore extremely difficult to fool them.

What the teacher transmits about character formation is what the teacher actually is.

The teacher is the actual model, and therefore, you have to be what you teach.

When a teacher is a fake, the students will know it right away.

It is so very important for a teacher to be able to say, "I do not know."

The importance of this cannot be overstressed. Pretending knowledge undermines not the knowledge but the character of the pupils.

Sometimes it is so much better to say, "Dear pupils, I myself am far from perfect in this point; and while I am teaching you, I myself am also trying to make some progress."

Beyond being fair and honest, it will also be respected by the children because then they will feel that they and the teacher are going somewhere together.

For how many among us can really say to our pupils, "Look at me, and behave exactly like this"?

The point is that certain things can be taught, or transmitted, by being a role model.

A teacher, by definition, is a model, and when a teacher has humility and integrity, they are transmitted.

And they are transmitted not only by personal example but also through the teacher's demands.

Many teachers create dishonesty, intellectual or otherwise, by their demands, as well as by what they give the better marks for—for instance, by giving a good mark to a dishonest paper, just because it is "nice."

But there is more to it than that.

It says in *Pirkei Avot* that Torah learning "endows him—the learner—with sovereignty and authority," or, in other words, what it means to master something and what it means not to master something.

Mastery means that one becomes the real owner, the real boss, of whatever it is that he studied.

And lack of mastery is the sloppiness that comes from not understanding what it means to do something, anything, properly.

This, in fact, may be the most important thing—learning the proper way of doing things.

If a teacher manages to cover all of the material in the curriculum, or more or less than that, it is not all that significant.

But if a teacher succeeds in teaching children how to do things properly, that is an achievement.

With time, such children will be able to close any gap.

To create a fine human being, even if that human being has less formal education than the average student in the other school—that is really worthwhile.

A rabbi is one who teaches others

There is a story in the Talmud of Elazar ben Durdia, a man who was such a sinner that there was hardly a single sin that he had not committed. One day he decided to repent.

He went about seeking help from the world.

He went to the hills and mountains and begged them to ask for mercy on his behalf.

The hills replied, "Before we ask for mercy for you, we must plead for mercy for ourselves."

He went to the Heavens and made a similar request. The Heavens also answered, "Before we ask for mercy for you, we have to plead for mercy for ourselves."

Elazar ben Durdia realized that the matter depended on his own repentance alone.

It is written that he placed his head between his knees and burst into such weeping and crying that his soul departed.

Then a voice from Heaven was heard, saying, "*Rabbi* Elazar ben Durdia is permitted to enter the life hereafter."

Extraordinary repentance arising out of great love heals and makes whole the totality of a personality.

There is no need for mortification and self-flagellation.

Primarily one has to live through the feeling of remorse.

The combination of longing and the knowledge of what is lacking to fill that longing is as much anguish as one can bear.

Everything is overturned.

Regarding Elazar ben Durdia, a student once asked, "It may be possible for the man to make an upheaval so sincerely that he experienced complete repentance, but how could he have become a rabbi so quickly? After all, a rabbi must be learned."

The reply to this was that a rabbi is one who teachers others.

When Elazar ben Durdia made his heartbreaking repentance, he became a teacher of many generations of penitents by showing them the way.

CHAPTER 23

Spiritual Direction

"These are pregnant times throughout the world. Just as in geology we have breaking lines between huge blocks of earth, so today we are at the juncture between great blocks of time. This is a place of storm and volcano—and of becoming."

The emphasis is not on specific qualities but on the right measure

It is important to realize that bad qualities are not of one sort—they are not absolute qualities.

They are more in the nature of modes of expression.

For example, while joy is certainly positive, an excess of good spirits is rather dangerous.

The emphasis is not on specific qualities but on right measure, on the correctness of application.

Even love and compassion can be bad when exercised without discrimination.

God made both the light and the darkness, the good and the evil.

Real battles of life

To conduct oneself properly in matters that are permitted is still fairly straightforward.

To do so with a degree of holiness is another matter.

One can be a scoundrel even within the bounds of the legally permitted in Torah, as the Ramban, a medieval sage, said.

It is a matter of how one eats and drinks, how one goes about one's affairs, even in the most intimate of life's details, where, in fact, the temptations are the greatest and the failures most common.

The struggles here, as the sages have frequently noted, are real battles of life, and the need to be careful and circumspect cannot be overstated.

There are transgressions that are so intrinsically habitual that they are no longer considered sinful.

The repetition makes them commonplace and acceptable.

What is shockingly bad the first time is no longer even perceived the tenth or twentieth time.

One has to be constantly on the alert

It is very difficult, if not impossible, to be certain about the lightness or severity of punishment for a particular transgression.

The essential question is, am I for God or against Him?

If one is against Him, then one is a rebel, and it doesn't make any difference whether it be a light charge or a severe charge.

And extenuating circumstances do not count. In war, men are killed for a trifle.

And in life, too, failure to perform a certain small duty may have very serious consequences.

One simply has to be constantly on the alert and attentive to all the possibilities.

At the moment of decision, one cannot determine to what extent a person merits punishment.

Only after the performance of the action can one distinguish its true nature, whether it belongs to the outer shell or the holiness.

One must learn the truth

It cannot be required of every person to learn all of the Torah or even to understand all of what is learned.

All that can be required is that whatever one does learn should be correct truth—not more or less or probable truth—but the kind of truth that will enable a person to be sure about which buttons he has to press and those that he has to avoid in an incompletely comprehended world.

It is not a matter of how much one knows but of how reliable and integral the knowledge is, no matter on what level.

Living for the sake of Heaven

A person may not be able to afford the luxuries of food and drink and yet, in a simple and innocent way, be guilty of gluttony by the mere fact that he is not eating for the sake of Heaven.

Similarly, a person may be clothed in gold and silk and partake of the greatest delicacies, but he may be doing so as a mode of Divine worship, in purity and in holiness.

Only through the body and the physical world can the genuinely spiritual be achieved

The Divine soul sees the body as an instrument, as a means that can serve the ends both of the unclean and of the holy.

According to the Jewish concept of things, physical things are not necessarily of a lower order, and the spiritual is not of itself something better.

An object can be material or spiritual without qualifying it as having any more or less value.

Much of Judaism rests on the practical *mitzvot,* which are quite simply actions performed in a certain way in the material world.

Mitzvot are not necessarily intended to be used as a means to gain the love of God or spiritual enlightenment for oneself.

They do not have any specific objective besides, perhaps, a union with God that is neither a spiritual nor a physical consummation.

Both the spiritual and the physical are at the same distance from the Divine, so that the question may legitimately be asked:

What does it matter to God whether one blesses a piece of bread or whether one smokes on the Sabbath?

Similarly, one may ask:

What harm can it do God to deny Him or to hate Him?

In terms of the Infinite, it is all on the same level of the inconsequential.

The human struggle is for the body and the use of the body.

What is one using the body for?

Is our physical neutral territory being lived in for the sake of God, and is the body mechanism expressing the yearning for God?

There is so much the body can perform.

It is said that only through the body, in any of a great many various modes of expression, can the genuinely spiritual be achieved.

Avoiding idolatry

Every Jew should be repulsed by idolatry.

The problem is to define idolatry properly.

When there is a doubt, an ignorance of what idolatry is, many Jews may be led astray to bring themselves, to a greater or lesser extent, to idolatry. In a manner of speaking, all of the Torah, as a whole, is an explanation of the first two commandments: "I am the Lord" and "Thou shalt have no other gods."

All the positive *mitzvot* are modes of contact with the one "I am."

The negative *mitzvot,* the prohibitions, can be considered as modes of avoiding severance from God.

Seen in this way, all that is required in following the Torah is a single, total sanctification of one's soul.

The important thing for everyone is to strive to remain connected.

But it seems that to scrape together enough force to break a single small habit is more difficult than to die a martyr's death on the pyre.

Such is the challenge of Israel—the readiness to give of oneself in small things as well as in big ones.

Contending with one's imagination

One of the things the person who is struggling with himself has to contend with is imagination, something that is not so easy to do.

Every thought, every fragment of thought and imagination, has its own force in the world of substance or of spirit. Just as the smallest trickle of water can make a deep impression on stone over a long period of time, thoughts affect the soul.

If a person entertains certain imaginings over a consistent period of time, they will become part of him. Just as diplomats are not retained for any considerable number of years in any ambassadorial post because they tend to become identified with their surroundings, so it is not healthy for any person to let his thoughts range over any of the realms of evil in casual imagination.

We have the recommendation to dwell on the greatness and goodness of God.

Even if this fulfills its purpose for only a moment or two, and one quickly returns to a normal state of forgetfulness, it may, by repetition, acquire the cumulative influence of habit.

The pitfalls of success

Suffering is a means of restoring a person to God.

As we have said, there are many who will never awaken to holiness without some life crisis.

Just as it is interesting to observe the effects of what is considered "success."

Not only does success often bring a certain crassness and insensitivity, but it also brings a forgetting of how to be grateful.

The sincere worshiper of God has to tighten the tension

The problem in a life of steady devotion and sincere worship lies in the fact that habit makes the tension slack.

Piety can become a comfortable state of being, in which one is afraid of change.

When arriving at such a stage, the sincere worshiper of God has to assume an additional burden, to tighten the tension.

Otherwise, he will slip into a state of gradual spiritual decline.

A better wine is far more difficult to appreciate

I have not found that accepting Judaism makes a life that is full of happiness and filled with sugar. It is not like this.

It doesn't make, by definition, a more enjoyable life. But it is a better life.

It is like drinking wine. There are the sweet wines that even children appreciate. They are very sweet. They are possibly not wine, but they are sweet. And red.

But a better wine is far more difficult to appreciate.

It is hard to teach about it. You have to experience it to understand that it is not as sweet and not as red and not as cheap but that it is still better.

It is something that one must educate oneself about.

Good cooking is not always appreciated. The better it is, the more you have to learn to appreciate it.

This is possibly true about every form of human achievement. To appreciate something that is better needs an education.

It needs a certain amount of suffering. But when you get there, you understand it.

This is exactly the time when one must not sleep

These are pregnant times throughout the world.

Just as in geology we have breaking lines between huge blocks of earth, so today we are at the juncture between great blocks of time.

This is a place of storm and volcano—and of becoming.

In today's reality, a small act can have far-reaching consequences, beyond imagination, whereas things that will be done five or ten years from today will be so much less effective.

This is precisely the meaning of pregnant times:

Anything can be born.

And this is exactly the time when one must not sleep.

NOTES

For each pebble in this book, I have attached a note. In most instances, the notes contain their own pebbles.

The notes consist mainly of references to places and passages in the published works of Rabbi Steinsaltz where the reader can see a similar or related idea for each pebble, usually in an expanded context.

Sometimes a note relates to some interesting detail within its pebble. While I do believe that the pebbles in this book are self-contained and have great value by themselves, I also recognize that they are part of a whole body of work and thought.

Many extraordinary books by Rabbi Steinsaltz are available in English; details of the ones cited here can be found in the Bibliography. It is my hope that these notes will serve to connect the pebbles with further study and exploration.

PART I: GOD

Chapter 1: Contemplating God

The decision to follow God p. 3

In trying to begin at the beginning, this first pebble is about God. Rabbi Steinsaltz writes,

"Jews are, in essence, in their fundamental quality, a theocentric people, a people for which God and the relationship to God, faith, and religion are a basic need of life, a primary one. For the Jewish people and for the individuals that compose it, faith, devotion, and ritual are not merely something that exists in their world, but a necessity that is derived from their very beginning" (*We Jews,* p. 133).

He also writes,

"Only when a man can relate his inner center to God as the first and foremost and only reality, only then does his self take on meaning" (*The Thirteen Petalled Rose,* p. 109).

Constantly standing before Him p. 3

In *We Jews,* Rabbi Steinsaltz writes about "the question of why so many Jews have been drawn to various faiths and religions, and why even in our generation, a large number of them, sometimes even more than 50% of believers, in new religions and cults, are Jews" (p. 137).

He goes on to say, "The person who has not received any preparation or followed any significant pathway to reach his Judaism, with all the challenges that it involves, finds himself, in the spiritual sense, in a tough situation. On the one hand, being a Jew, he feels a deep need to identify with religious faith, an inward need for religion and cultic ritual. At the same time, the Jewish religion seems strange and incomprehensible to him, and the path toward it is difficult" (ibid.).

This pebble suggests an approach to meditation that centers on an intellectual contemplation of the Infinite. Rabbi Steinsaltz explores this Jewish form of meditation throughout *The Long Shorter Way;* see, for example, chapter 5, "The Way of Understanding," and chapter 41, "Awe and Fear of God."

Awareness of the Divine presence p. 4

I once heard Rabbi Steinsaltz say, "I never saw it written that to be a Jew you have to have a lobotomy." In *The Thirteen Petalled Rose,* Rabbi Steinsaltz writes, "We are even able to increase our receptivity to holiness by *opening ourselves* to its influence" (p. 51). Rabbi Steinsaltz also writes, "The surrender of oneself on the Sabbath is not simply a matter of non-activity but of *opening oneself* to the influence of the higher worlds and thereby receiving the strength for all the days of the week that follow" (p. 57).

Meditating on the Divine p. 4

Rabbi Steinsaltz has written more about this in several places. See, for example, *The Long Shorter Way,* where Rabbi Steinsaltz expands on the themes of love and awe of God. See in particular chapter 41, "Awe and Fear of God," and chapter 44, "Two Ways of Loving God."

Contemplating God's greatness p. 5

Rabbi Steinsaltz once said to me, "We are planting trees, not vegetables." As Rabbi Steinsaltz writes, "Though a person may be acutely conscious of the moment of repentance, the knowledge can come later. It is in fact rare for repentance to take the form of a sudden, dramatic conversion, and it generally takes the form of *a series of small turnings*" (*The Thirteen Petalled Rose*, p. 96).

Awareness requires inner growth p. 5

Rabbi Steinsaltz uses the same point of departure in his chapter "Repentance" in *The Thirteen Petalled Rose.* He writes, "The essence of repentance has frequently been found in the poetic lines of the *Song of Songs,* 'The King had brought me to his chambers' (1:4). This verse has been interpreted as meaning that he whose search has reached a certain level feels that he is in the palace of the King. He goes from room to room, from hole to hole, seeking Him out. However, the King's Palace is an endless series of worlds, and as a man proceeds in his search from room to room, he holds only the end of the string. It is, nevertheless, a continuous going, and going after God, a going to God, day after day year after year" (p. 99).

Parables with the use of the King also appear in *The Tales of Rabbi Nachman of Bratslav,* in which Rabbi Steinsaltz retells and offers commentary on six important tales of the Hasidic master Rabbi Nachman.

Focusing and clinging to God p. 6

In *A Guide to Jewish Prayer,* chapter 5, Rabbi Steinsaltz writes, "There is a well-known dictum stressing the importance of *kavvanah:* 'Prayer without *kavvanah* is like a body without a soul.' This means that prayer, which is the speech addressed by man to his Creator, loses its essential quality when it becomes solely the recitation of words, without *inward attention to the meaning of the words being spoken*" (p. 34).

For more on the concept of *kavvanah*, see chapter 5, "*Kavvanah.*"

God is not an abstraction but an actuality p. 6

In an essay called "Kabbalah for Today" (see http://www.steinsaltz.org), Rabbi Steinsaltz writes,

"Today, most of us are simply incapable of comprehending Kabbalah. For us the question is, 'Is there some way we, too, can "receive" the remarkable teachings of Kabbalah in a meaningful way, without treading upon its divine essence?'

"One answer lies in the Hasidic approach to Kabbalah.

"It is a basic Kabbalistic concept that the human soul is, in a manner of speaking, a spark of Divine revelation within the world and that each human being is a microcosm of the entire universe. Hasidism shows how the rarified teachings of Kabbalah, which speak to the macro-universe, can be adapted into a structure with ethical and practical meaning for our individual lives.

"In this way, Hasidism is a form of applied Kabbalah. Just as the Revealed Law frames the behavior of our bodies, the internalization of Kabbalistic notions of the Hidden Law can attune us to our soul, educating it to connect with the Divine. In this model, the power of Kabbalah is harnessed not to serve our own desires but to align them with the wishes of the Almighty."

Chapter 2: The Inconceivable God

God is that which cannot be grasped p. 9

In *The Thirteen Petalled Rose,* Rabbi Steinsaltz writes, "The Infinite is beyond anything that can be grasped in any terms—either positive or negative. Not only is it impossible to say of the Infinite that He is in any way limited or that He is bad, one cannot even say the opposite, that He is vast or He is good. Just as He is not matter, He is not spirit, nor can He be said to exist in any dimension meaningful to us. The dilemma posed by this meaning of infinity is more than a consequence of the inadequacy of the mind. It represents a simply unbridgeable gap, a gap that cannot be crossed by anything definable" (p. 26).

The Divine essence fills everything p. 10

Here are a few lines from *The Thirteen Petalled Rose* also concerning God's Oneness, as well as the multiplicity of our world. Rabbi Steinsaltz explores the use of the image of "screens" in this context:

"An archetypal representation of a 'screen' is the curtain dividing the humanly sacred from the Holy of Holies in the holy Temple. . . . This idea of a screen is only an image to explain the essence of the differences among all things. In the world of emanation, in the Godhead, there are no such barriers and the unity is complete. In order for a world to exist separate from the Godhead, there has to be a contraction of the highest essence. This contraction of infinite wisdom, or withdrawal of divine plenty, is therefore the basis for the creation of the universe; and the screen—representing the hiddenness of the divine—is the basis for making the worlds manifest as separate worlds" (p. 17).

There is nothing other than God p. 10

Rabbi Steinsaltz writes in *The Thirteen Petalled Rose,* "Precisely because the Divine is apprehended as an infinite, not a finite, force, everything in the cosmos, whether small or large, is only a small part of the pattern, so that there is no difference in weight or gravity between any one part and another. The movement of a man's finger is as important or unimportant as the most terrible catastrophe, for as against the Infinite both are of the same dimension. Just as the Infinite can be defined as unlimited in the sense of being *beyond* everything, so He can be defined as being close to and touching everything" (p. 34).

There is no before or after in God p. 11

See *Simple Words* for Rabbi Steinsaltz's essay titled "God." *Simple Words* also includes an essay titled "Good Deeds."

This essay was based on a lecture in which Rabbi Steinsaltz said, "Unlike the biggest of bosses, God is infinite. Infinity is a difficult concept, even in mathematics. In relation to God, it is more difficult yet. Something infinite has no boundaries. There is no limit to the number of details it can contain."

In the essay "Good Deeds," Rabbi Steinsaltz explores, among other things, the relationship of the infinite God to the tiniest of details in the world.

To God, there is no large or small p. 11

In *We Jews,* Rabbi Steinsaltz writes, "Belief in God includes from the start, beginning with the Ten Commandments, two components that everyone finds difficult to grasp and to identify with. The first is the perception of God as the One and Only, who is therefore all-embracing and all-supreme, divine, above all comprehension, and therefore far above any personal relationship to something defined and specific. To this is compounded another difficulty, which is a faith that is entirely an abstraction, which does not allow any image, form, or other experience that can be grasped" (pp. 134–135).

How can one speak about the unspeakable? p. 12

For Rabbi Steinsaltz's essential essay on the subject of the holy, see "Holiness" in *The Thirteen Petalled Rose.*

Rabbi Steinsaltz writes, "The root meaning of the concept of 'the holy' in the holy language is separation: it implies the apartness and remoteness of something. The holy is that which is out of bounds, untouchable, and altogether beyond grasp; it cannot be understood or even defined, being so totally unlike anything else. To be holy is, in essence, to be distinctly other" (p. 51).

There are no words to describe the Transcendent p. 13

Further exploration of the subject of "light" can be found in Rabbi Steinsaltz's essay "The Motif of Light in the Jewish Tradition" in *On Being Free*. Rabbi Steinsaltz writes, "Light, fundamentally, does not belong to this world; it is rather an emanation of a different essence, from the other side of reality. . . . Divine revelation itself is a revelation of light" (pp. 181–182).

The infinite light of God has no limit p. 14

Rabbi Steinsaltz deals with the same challenge in *The Thirteen Petalled Rose:* "There are many things in the world, such as numbers, that may have infinity as one of the attributes and yet also be limited either in function or purpose or in their very nature. But when we speak of the Infinite, Blessed be He, we mean the utmost of perfection and abstraction, that which encompasses everything and is beyond all possible limits" (p. 25).

Nothing can occur without God p. 15

Teachings and reference to the Baal Shem Tov, Rabbi Yisrael ben Eliezer (d. 1760), the founder of the Hasidic movement, can be found in a number of places in Rabbi Steinsaltz's multivolume commentary on the *Tanya.*

In *Learning from the Tanya,* for example, Rabbi Steinsaltz writes, "The students of the Baal Shem Tov said, 'When we studied Torah with the Baal Shem Tov, it was with thunder and lightning and the sound of the *shofar,* as it was when the Torah was given on Mt. Sinai, when "all the people saw the thunder . . . and the nation feared and moved and stood from afar."' The Mt. Sinai experience was a transcendental experience, beyond the boundaries of time and space, existing forever. Like the creation of the world, it is a permanent state, not a one-time act but an ongoing activity. Whenever one sits and studies Torah properly, [one] hears the voice of God" (p. 213).

Words like "I" and "mine" become meaningless p. 16

In *The Thirteen Petalled Rose,* Rabbi Steinsaltz discusses the cosmos of reality as worlds upon worlds and says, "The lower the world, the more it is pervaded by a sense of the 'I'—and consequently the more it is subject to the obscuring of the divine essence" (p. 15).

To exist beyond the apparent limits of reality p. 16

In *Understanding the Tanya,* Rabbi Steinsaltz discusses time in another way: "Time does not change God. He is today as He was yesterday and as He was before the world was created" (p. 58).

And in *The Thirteen Petalled Rose*, when describing the significance of time in other worlds, Rabbi Steinsaltz writes, "Indeed, upon ascending the order of worlds, this time system becomes increasingly abstract and less and less representative of anything that we know as time in the physical world; it becomes no more than the purest essence of change, or even of the possibility of potential change" (p. 4).

A God I can put into my pocket is not worth being with p. 17

In *A Guide to Jewish Prayer,* Rabbi Steinsaltz writes, "God as father, close and intimate, and God as exalted and majestic Being—which seem to be at opposing poles of religious experience—are united in the world of Judaism. Indeed, the combined presence is in itself a fundamental principle in the Jewish worldview. As the poet says, 'Further than any distance and nearer than any nearness,' or, 'Where ever I find You, You are concealed in evanescence, and where ever I do not find You, Your glory fills the earth.' This dual conception, known in philosophy as the combination of the transcendental and the immanent view of the Divine, and referred to in the Kabbalah as the tension between the aspects of God as 'surrounding all worlds' and 'permeating all worlds,' is an essential element of the inner truth of Judaism, and constitutes a central issue in every work of Jewish thought. Any examination of Jewish faith relates to this issue either directly or indirectly. The Kabbalistic appellation of God—'the Infinite, Blessed be He'—in itself reflects this double aspect of the Divine, combining an abstract, distancing term alongside one of nearness and human concern" (p. 12).

Chapter 3: Looking for God

God hides Himself p. 19

Rabbi Steinsaltz writes in *The Thirteen Petalled Rose,* "It can be said that all of the worlds—and, indeed, any separate realms of being—exist only by virtue of the fact that God makes Himself hidden. . . . A world can exist only as a result of the concealment of its Creator" (p. 15).

Confronting a paradox p. 20

Rabbi Steinsaltz, in *The Thirteen Petalled Rose,* writes, "God hides Himself, putting aside his essential infiniteness and withholding His endless light to the extent necessary in order that the world may exist. Within the actual Divine light nothing can maintain its own existence; the world becomes possible only through the special act of Divine withdrawal or contraction. Such Divine non-being, or concealment, is thus the necessary condition for the existence of that which is finite" (p. 26).

God hides, and we look for Him p. 20

In *Learning from the Tanya,* Rabbi Steinsaltz writes, "All of existence receives from only one Source, that One besides Whom nothing exists. . . . Creation is inextricably intertwined with constriction. And because there is constriction and concealment of God's countenance, it is possible for beings to exist in which the Divine is hidden, beings that see the Divine speech as, at most, a first cause of their being but that do not comprehend how God is literally giving life to the universe, how His speech directly creates every being without an intermediary, at every moment, literally from nothingness" (pp. 180–181).

God conceals Himself so that man shall seek and find Him p. 21

In *Understanding the Tanya,* Rabbi Steinsaltz writes, "Our reality is considered the lowest world because the concealment of the divine is here most pronounced, the darkness is doubled and redoubled, and the divine light is completely shaded. More precisely, ours is the lowest world in which the concealed divine light can still be revealed; it is the lowest world that can still be uplifted" (p. 218).

God hides, but few seek p. 22

Another story about a grandfather and grandson that Rabbi Steinsaltz retells is this:

"Constriction creates a world of concealment. . . . For such a reality to exist, there must be a vast distance between us and God, and a dense concealment of his presence; for if we were to be directly aware of the divine presence in everything, then there would be no more world. The reality of this world is a play of light and shadow, of revelation and concealment of the divine light. . . . In the last moments of Rabbi Schneur Zalman's life, as he was fleeing Napoleon and taking refuge in a cabin in an out-of-the-way Russian village called Pyena, he asked his grandson, 'What do you see?' His grandson replied, 'I see the cabin, the wooden wall, the beam in the ceiling.' Rabbi Schneur Zalman answered him, 'And at this moment, I only see divinity.'

"A person who sees only divinity is no longer a participant in the game of the world. For him, the world is no longer a world, for it no longer conceals divinity. Even the greatest *tzaddikim* need at least the possibility of not seeing the divinity directly. That clear sight will constitute the reality of the end of days, when people will see that 'This is our God!' Then there will no longer be any meaning to concepts such as free will or eternal life. The present structure will melt away and lose all its meaning, and the world will become a transformed reality where nothing is hidden" (*Learning from the Tanya,* p. 170).

Our perception of God is limited by physical existence p. 22

Rabbi Steinsaltz, in his *Tanya* commentary, writes, "The world and God are always in opposition; because they are an essential contradiction, it makes them unable to coexist. They can exist together only when God is hidden, as it were, only when the world does not know and sense that divine essence. In other words, the existence of every world is a fiction, and it can continue to exist only as long as it is not aware of that. At the moment that it realizes that it is a fiction, it ceases to be.

The divine light must be concealed 'in order that they should not dissolve out of existence'" (*Understanding the Tanya,* pp. 221–222).

The development of the world requires darkness p. 23

Rabbi Steinsaltz defines *tzimtzum* as "contraction." The glossary of Rabbi Steinsaltz's commentary on the Tanya defines *tzimtzum* as "a basic Kabbalistic concept that refers to the contraction and limitation of *Ein Sof,* which provides room for the creation of all the worlds." Rabbi Steinsaltz defines *Ein Sof* as "the Infinite One." He continues by saying, "A term in Kabbalah that refers to God as He exists above and beyond every limitation and definition. Although the term is only a negative characterization of God, it constitutes a kind of definition, and hence it cannot be accepted as a characterization of God's essential being, which is above all definition, even by negation. Instead, we understand the term as a characterization of the first emanation from God's essential being, an emanation that is sometimes referred to as His Name. Because the relation between this first emanation and God's essence is comparable to the relation between the light of the sun and the body of the sun, this first emanation is often referred to as *Ohr Ein Sof,* 'the Infinite Light'" (*Learning from the Tanya,* p. 303).

An expression of God's infinite power p. 24

On the attraction to making a concrete image of "God," Rabbi Steinsaltz writes, "The unified whole of an entity that is above and beyond comprehension is infinitely distant, and therefore infinitely difficult to conceive of and to identify with. Another aspect of this difficulty of abstraction is the most basic prohibition against creating a statue or image. The statue or image, the fetish, has an enormous advantage from the emotional viewpoint. It is a thing that a person, at nearly any level, can relate to. Something that can be imagined as a concrete structure, that can be seen, sensed, touched, is capable of realization and closeness. The god that has a specific definition, that takes a human form—the image of a man, his desires—seems far closer and simpler, and can be loved in a concrete and sensual manner" (*We Jews,* p. 135).

Only God can cross the abyss p. 24

"There would, therefore, seem to be an abyss stretching between God and the world—and not only the physical world of time, space, and gravity, but also the spiritual worlds, no matter how sublime, defined as each one is within the boundaries of its own definition. Creation itself becomes divine paradox. To bridge the abyss, the infinite keeps creating the world. His creation being not the act of forming something out of nothing but the act of revelation. Creation is an emanation from the divine light; its secret is not the coming into existence of something new but the transmutation of the divine reality into something defined and limited—into a world. This transmutation involves a process, or a mystery, of contraction" (*The Thirteen Petalled Rose,* p. 26).

God continuously sustains the world p. 25

This view, that God did not create the world but rather is constantly creating and sustaining the world, is explored in "Divine Manifestation," chapter 2 of *The Thirteen Petalled Rose:* "Even though it appears as an entity in itself, the world is formed and sustained by the divine power" (p. 27). And in the chapter "Torah" in *The Thirteen Petalled Rose,* Rabbi Steinsaltz writes that the material world "is the marvel of Creation for the paradoxical reason that the very existence of matter is a condition that seems to obscure the Divine, and thus could only be the result of a special intention on the part of the Infinite. Matter is a sort of standing wave between the manifestation of God and the hiddenness of God; it is defined by its limitations. To retain separate and independent existence, infinite force has to be exerted on every particle" (p. 69).

The adventure of finding God behind the partition p. 26

In *Understanding the Tanya,* Rabbi Steinsaltz writes, "When a person is immersed in Torah and *mitzvot,* his soul is liberated from the bonds of the body and clings to God. The soul can experience no greater joy than that" (p. 107).

Chapter 4: Knowing God

Removing the sensory images that prevent one from seeing p. 27

In the essay "Why Are Our People Involved in Idolatry?" in *We Jews*, Rabbi Steinsaltz writes, "The evil inclination of idolatry is thus the outcome of a conflict between the deep need for religion, faith, and serving God, and the human difficulty of creating a relationship with an abstraction. This conflict, this tension, is what creates the temptation to satisfy the longing for the divine with something perverse—that is, by means of idolatry, cultic ritual, and devotion to something simpler and easier for human beings. It is thus that the urge towards faith takes the form of idolatry" (p. 136).

To what extent am I conscious of God's presence? p. 28

"To be sure, it takes both time and considerable introspection to get beyond the elaborate mental constructions, the words and ideas, devised by everyone. Often, too, a person will feel that he can make do with partial pragmatic answers, that he has as much as he can handle just coping with the necessities of the everyday" (*The Thirteen Petalled Rose,* p. 104).

God is not to be found in some other world p. 28

In *Understanding the Tanya,* Rabbi Steinsaltz writes, "One *tzaddik* observed that when heaven decides to cast a person down, he is presented with doubtful thoughts about the *tzaddikim.* When he falls further, he is presented with doubts about his friends. Thus, it sometimes happens that a person's relationship with a friend, brother, or relative changes for no reason, as though something has shifted, a part of the soul has been poisoned, and things cannot go back to what they had been. He entertains suspicions, and the more he suspects, the more they grow, until a wall arises that separates him from the other person (in the spiritual realm, a wall can arise that separates him from God). And that wall cannot be fixed—it can only be broken down" (p. 71).

In the presence of God p. 29

This basic assumption, that "one who does not struggle is not a servant of God," is a major thread in Part II of this book. Avoiding struggle is not the goal; the goal is endless struggle and one's strategy under those circumstances.

A very clear message is always being transmitted p. 31

Similarly, Rabbi Steinsaltz writes, in *The Thirteen Petalled Rose,* regarding God's question to Adam, "Where are you?": "The Voice in the garden is still reverberating throughout the world, and it is still heard, not always openly or in full consciousness but nevertheless still heard, in one way or another, in a person's soul" (p. 106).

Recognizing the obvious p. 31

See Rabbi Steinsaltz's comment in chapter 1 of *The Thirteen Petalled Rose,* titled "Worlds," where, in his discussion of how we humans are creating angels all the time, he writes, "The creation of an angel in our world and the immediate relegation of this angel to another world is, in itself, not at all a supernatural phenomenon; it is a part of the familiar realm of experience, an integral piece of life, which may even seem ordinary and commonplace, because of its traditional rootedness in the system of *mitzvot,* or the order of sanctity. When we are in the act of creating the angel, we have no perception of the angel being created, and this act seems to be a part of the whole structure of the practical material world in which we live (p. 10).

A sharp consciousness of Divinity p. 32

In *Understanding the Tanya,* Rabbi Steinsaltz writes, "When the *Shekhinah* dwells within a person, place, or situation, he or it can no longer exist as an independent entity. Nothing can maintain its individuality and still be an instrument for the revelation of the *Shekhinah.* For the purposes of that divine revelation, the vessel must be transparent. If a person sees himself as a something, he is at that moment closed off (fully or in part) from the illumination, and the divine light cannot rest on him. The divine Being can be revealed through a person or an object only if he or it is a nonbeing, lacking existence.

"This is not to say that a person who falls short of this ideal is necessarily cut off from the *Shekhinah* but rather that a barrier exists, that his personal existence stands between him and God.

"God is to be found everywhere. However, as long as something possesses a certain independent existence, it cannot be a vessel for the divine revelation. A person can still serve his Maker, doing His will and agency (since in a sense everything in one way or another, in the great scope of existence, performs God's will). However, he cannot be a vessel on which the *Shekhinah* rests and through which the *Shekhinah* is revealed" (pp. 197–198).

In *Understanding the Tanya,* Rabbi Steinsaltz also writes, "A person is like a candle—'the candle of the Lord is the soul of the person' (Proverbs 20:27). The wick of that candle is the body, and the fire is the light of the *Shekhinah*" (p. 191). One of Rabbi Steinsaltz's books is titled *The Candle of God*.

Revelation is the recognition of a reality that was overlooked p. 32

"The Holy One is discovered to be beyond all this; He is immanent and flows within life, in the passage from one world to another. . . . There is no above or below in approaching Him" (*The Thirteen Petalled Rose,* p. 81).

God is always present p. 33

"Remoteness from God is, of course, not a matter of physical distance, but a spiritual problem of relationship. The person who is not going along the right path is not farther away from God but is, rather, a man whose soul is oriented toward and relating with other objects. The starting point of repentance is precisely this fulcrum point upon which a person turns himself about, away from the pursuit of what he craves, and confronts his desire to approach God; this is the moment of conversion, the crucial moment of repentence" (*The Thirteen Petalled Rose,* p. 96).

A source of inspiration and joy to those able to grasp it p. 34

Regarding effort and commitment, it reminds me that Rabbi Steinsaltz writes in the chapter "The Search for Oneself" in *The Thirteen Petalled Rose,* "To be sure, it takes both time and considerable introspection to get beyond the elaborate mental constructions, the words and ideas, devised by everyone" (p. 104). Also, in his chapter "Repentance," Rabbi Steinsaltz writes, "As he liberates himself from alien influences, the penitent can only gradually straighten himself out; he has to overcome the forms engraved by time and place before he can reach his own image" (p. 95).

Speaking with God p. 34

This pebble, with reference to Rabbi Steinsaltz's daughter, reminds me that of all the passages in my book *On the Road with Rabbi Steinsaltz,* the part that has prompted the most enthusiastic comments by far is the conversation between Rabbi Steinsaltz and my daughter, Miriam, on the subject of love, relationships, and romance.

Chapter 5: Intimacy

Some people feel an intimacy with God p. 37

As Rabbi Steinsaltz points out in one of the answers to the series of nine questions posed to him at the end of his book *The Tales of Rabbi Nachman of Bratslav,* "Much of what has been written about Rabbi Nachman is connected with the fact that he was, on the one hand, very open to describing his moods, his thoughts, and his ideas to the people around him, and the fact that his disciples wrote down almost anything they could remember of his utterances" (p. 285). The introduction to the book, as well as the answers Rabbi Steinsaltz offers to the nine questions, adds significant insight into Rabbi Nachman.

The constant presence of God p. 37

A part of chapter 34 in *Understanding the Tanya* deals with divine unity. "God is found in everything, filling and transcending all being. But not everything that exists feels it. There are, however, rare individuals . . . and there was also once a special place, the established place for His habitation, where God's unity was revealed—the Temple. But with the destruction of the Temple, God has no other instrument to reveal His unity in the world. . . . The divine unity is revealed in the four cubits of *halakhah.* There, a person can connect and unite with God, coming as close to Him as possible" (pp. 168–169).

God is closer than the beating of one's heart p. 38

In *The Thirteen Petalled Rose,* Rabbi Steinsaltz writes, "The contact and mutual attraction between body and soul creates a contingency, a unique situation, generating the human self, which is neither body nor soul but a merging of the two. This conjoined self can achieve great things, giving expression to the glory of the body in being raised from the inertness of matter and to the exhilaration of the soul's response to this mutual contact" (p. 42).

God wants a living relationship p. 39

In *The Thirteen Petalled Rose,* Rabbi Steinsaltz writes, "When a man learns that just as he broods over himself so does God yearn for him and look for him, he is at the beginning of a higher level of consciousness. From this moment he can begin to follow the guiding strings that are leading him, usually with enormous toil and labor, toward the focal point of himself. For in truth it is not one question with two sides but a meeting place of two questions, that of man seeking himself and of God seeking man" (p. 110).

God reaches out to us p. 40

"God, precisely because God in His being infinitely distant, beyond any possible contact, is Himself the one who creates the ways, the means of contact, in which every thought, every tremor of anticipation and desire on the part of man work their way until they reach the Holy One Himself, the Infinite, Blessed be He" (*The Thirteen Petalled Rose,* p. 35).

Permitting God to enter p. 41

Also about the Kotzker Rebbe, Rabbi Steinsaltz writes, "Each of us must make moral choices as to how we will conduct ourselves. The Torah permits marital relations, yet a person can, while acting wholly within the framework of the law, indulge a greedy lust born of unrestrained desire. The Torah allows the consumption of meat and wine, yet a person may, while eating only kosher foods (even simple food, and as he exercises proper table manners), become obsessed with gratifying his palate. Or someone may be honest, yet immersed in the pursuit of money with such utter self-abandon that it becomes his personal idol. In this sense, the Kotzker Rebbe states that a person can commit adultery with his own wife" (*Understanding the Tanya,* pp. 86–87).

We are permanently connected to God p. 42

In *Learning from the Tanya,* Rabbi Steinsaltz writes, "The basis of the Jewish character has two related qualities. First is clinging to God, and the second is repulsion from any form of idolatry. Clinging to God is expressed in the first of the Ten Commandments, 'I am the Lord your God'; and repulsion from idolatry is expressed in the second commandment: 'You shall not have any other gods.' . . . These two commandments comprise more than the distillation of the Torah; they are the essence of the soul of every Jew" (pp. 144–145).

The process of creation is continuous p. 42

This same theme is discussed in many of the pebbles in Part I of this book. In the chapter titled "Divine Manifestation" in *The Thirteen Petalled Rose,* Rabbi Steinsaltz writes, "An old allegory illustrates this influence by depicting the world as a small island in the middle of the sea, inhabited by birds. To provide them with sustenance, the kingdom has arranged an intricate network of channels through which the necessary food and water flow. So long as the birds behave as they are endowed by nature to behave, singing and soaring through the air, the flow of plenty proceeds without interruption. But when the birds begin to play in the dirt and peck at the channels, the channels get blocked or broken and cease to function properly, and the flow from above is disrupted. So, too, does the island that is our world depend on the proper functioning of the *Sefirot;* and when they are interfered with, the system is disrupted, and the disrupting factors themselves suffer the consequences" (p. 29).

The simple human emotion of gratitude p. 43

Rabbi Steinsaltz's commentary on the Passover Haggadah includes insight into the Grace After Meals. Rabbi Steinsaltz writes, "The expression of gratitude for the food we have eaten is one of the most fundamental of all human (and apparently not only human) responses, and, as a result, it is also one that can easily be lost; cognitive and other responses are likely to disrupt it" (*The Passover Haggadah*).

Awakening the natural impulse to love God p. 44

Rabbi Steinsaltz writes, "It is told of the author of *Tanya* that he would stand in meditation and declare before God: 'I do not want Your *Gan Eden,* I do not want Your world to come—I only want You!' There is a level on which a person attains a lofty state and desires to delight in God, so he is given the chance to delight in God. But higher than this is the level on which a person desires nothing. He waives even the pleasure that is found in the love of God and wants only 'to [be] drawn into the body of the King'—to negate himself completely within God" (*Opening the Tanya,* p. 240).

Nothing should interfere with acts of gratitude to God p. 44

In his "Introduction to the Blessing After Meals" in *The Miracle of the Seventh Day,* Rabbi Steinsaltz writes, "We give thanks for what we have enjoyed from the world that God has given us. Like all blessings of Thanksgiving, the Blessing After Meals expresses a very basic emotion: the acknowledgment of kindness. This feeling is general, and even goes beyond the human realm, for animals, too, recognized the kindness done to them by their benefactors. The sages commented that this is how Abraham would bring his visitors closer to the service of God: when they thanked him for the food they had eaten in his home, he would tell them that they ought also to acknowledge the source of all goodness" (p. 179).

A genuine fear of God p. 45

"Love and fear are not necessarily incompatible, for any love contains, within itself, fear. Whenever there is an object of love, there is also the fear of losing it. This is not fear of punishment but fear of being disconnected from God. 'Fear that is contained in love' is, in a sense, the highest level of the fear of God, located where love and fear intertwine. It is the foundation and distillation of Jewish life. When we love, we cling to and are absorbed into the Source of life. When we fear, we are afraid that we may be severed from that Source—which would mean that we were no longer alive" (*Learning from the Tanya,* p. 139).

One fears God because one feels Him p. 45

"The sages discuss two levels of fear. The first is 'lower fear,' regarding which it was said, 'If there is no fear, there is no wisdom.' Without fear, there is no possibility of studying Torah. In order to study Torah properly, we must relate to it as the Torah of God. To do so, we must begin with a simple and basic fear of God, which will make it possible to then receive God's wisdom. The second level is 'higher fear.' Regarding this, our sages said, 'If there is no wisdom, there is no fear.' This is a fear that we attain through wisdom. . . . In order to draw it down to ourselves, we must be wise in Torah and understand what it means to study 'all these statutes' that God has commanded us" (*Learning from the Tanya,* p. 213).

Chapter 6: Faith

The path of faith p. 47

Read the first few essays in the book *On Being Free* by Rabbi Steinsaltz. The title essay and the three that follow it ("Freedom Without Content," "The First Step," and "The Question of Jewish Identity"), like this pebble, build on the consciousness of slavery in Egypt, the urge for freedom, and the paradoxical discovery that the path of faith is the path of freedom.

Getting stuck with infantile images of God p. 48

Rabbi Steinsaltz writes, "One of the special things about the Jews is a certain mental quality that undoubtedly exists in other nations, but is more predominant among us, and this is the inclination toward idolatry. . . . The essential nature of this inclination toward idolatry, toward the desire for it and the devotion to it, can be understood as the other side, the dark side, of the basic characteristic of the people of Israel, the power of faith that it possesses" (*We Jews,* p. 133).

God really does exist p. 49

Rabbi Steinsaltz writes, "The people of Israel is essentially a people that has not only a hold on its religion, but a very deep spiritual need, a very basic one, for faith" (*We Jews,* p. 133).

The power of faith p. 49

Rabbi Steinsaltz writes, "Israel, as our sages say, is a nation of 'believers who are the sons of believers'" (*We Jews,* p. 133).

Faith is given to us as an inheritance p. 50

Rabbi Steinsaltz writes, "There is a holiness that is inherited, that belongs to the family, given by God" (*The Thirteen Petalled Rose,* p. 60).

Faith is the key that ensures the joy of life p. 50

Rabbi Steinsaltz writes, "The awareness that God is with a person whatever his personal fate may be (whether he is righteous or wicked, wealthy or poor, happy or unfortunate) creates a fundamental joy" (*Understanding the Tanya,* p. 152).

Doubt is always present p. 51

Rabbi Steinsaltz writes, "As the sages have said, there is no attribute that lacks its injurious aspect, its negation and failure, just as there is no attribute—even if connected with doubt and heresy—that has not, under some circumstance, its holy aspect" (*The Thirteen Petalled Rose,* p. 77).

Most concepts of belief are acquired in the kindergarten years p. 51

"As he liberates himself from alien influences, the penitent can only gradually straighten himself out; he has to overcome the forms engraved by time and place before he can reach his own image. He must break free of the chains, the limitations, and the restrictions imposed by environment and education" (*The Thirteen Petalled Rose*, p. 95).

Paradoxes, unanswered problems, and logical contradictions p. 52

Not infrequently, Rabbi Steinsaltz uses examples from mathematics. In *The Thirteen Petalled Rose,* he writes, as part of his explanation of the abstract concept of "space," "Perhaps one may compare it to those self-contained systems—known in mathematics as 'groups' or 'fields'—in each of which all the unit parts are related in a definite way to the other parts and to the whole" (p. 3). And interestingly, Rabbi Steinsaltz, as part of his explanation of why Jews face Jerusalem when we pray, writes, "Rabbi Schneur Zalman of Lyady writes in his halakhic work, known as *Shulkhan Arukh ha-Rav,* that in order to establish the exact direction it is necessary to use spheric trigonometry" (*A Guide to Jewish Prayer,* p. 291).

The recognition of a Higher Power is not a matter of faith p. 52

Rabbi Steinsaltz writes, "The belief in one God is not merely an abstract statement about some kind of reality that exists outside of ourselves. It also implies the supremacy of this single essential entity within all reality: all particularities, with all their differences and divisions, are unified and subject to a single authority. In this regard, every monistic perception is a kind of comprehensive statement—even if not in religious language—of the very same thing, that is to say, the presupposition of the existence of a unified essence from which the different particularities are constructed and are given significance" (*We Jews,* p. 159).

The way to faith is never smooth p. 53

A point stressed in *The Thirteen Petalled Rose* is the unique nature of each person's path. "In the last resort the relationship to the Divine is individual" (p. 35). And "there exists, whether he acknowledges it or not, a path that is his own" (p. 96). And "each person can discover the special lines of his own direction" (p. 110).

The Torah does not command us to believe in God p. 54

When asked, "What is faith?" Rabbi Steinsaltz said, "I can say in a concise way that there is a theorem in mathematics, in projective geometry, called Desargues' theorem. It is an easy theorem to understand. Any schoolchild can understand it. But it is impossible to prove it—until one introduces a point in the infinite. Once you imagine a point in the infinite, the theorem can be proved. It is the same in our world. To begin to understand it, we must imagine the infinite" (*On the Road with Rabbi Steinsaltz,* p. 113).

There is a gladness in Heaven when man passes the Divine test p. 55

An extraordinary set of fourteen chapters comprise a section of Rabbi Steinsaltz's book *The Candle of God* titled "The Trials of Life." In these profound teachings, the theme of the Divine test is explored in some depth. Rabbi Steinsaltz writes, "The trials and tribulations of life are for the good. This does not mean that they are pleasant; there does exist a certain gap between the two. The point is that God tests a person in order to bring him to a higher level of knowledge. There may be said to be five aspects of being tested: the trial of sorrow and pain, the trial of disappointment, the trial of faith, the trial of hope, and the trial of expectation. Each one of these is a testing experience of its own kind" (p. 213).

PART II: THE SEEKER
Chapter 7: The Soul

The ways in which the soul is clothed p. 59

In his essay "The Psychology of the Soul," Rabbi Steinsaltz writes, "The image used in earlier Kabbalistic and Hasidic works to describe the revealing is that of 'garbing.' The distinction between the two concepts, 'garbing' and 'revealing,' is extremely important. The implication of revealing in this sense in which it is normally used is that the entity itself, in its essence, is made apparent, is uncovered, and that there is no intermediary between it and the perceiver. 'Garbing,' on the other hand, refers to a situation in which there is precisely such an intermediary, a 'garment.' The garment is a separate entity, although it generally possesses no character or personality of its own: it serves as an instrument, whose function is to reveal the nature and the goal of another entity" (*The Strife of the Spirit,* pp. 55–56).

The soul clothes itself in the blood of man p. 59

The entire essay just cited, "The Psychology of the Soul," is a further exploration of how the metaphor of clothing and garbing is used in Hasidic thought.

The soul may be likened to a person driving a car p. 60

Similarly, "The relation between body and soul, and altogether between the spirit of things and their corporeality, may be expressed by the example of a rider on horseback. A rider who is in control and guides his steed can go much farther than he can go on foot. How aptly then does the image of the Messiah as a poor man riding on a donkey describe the human predicament; the divine spark borne and guiding, the physical donkey bearing up and waiting for guidance and power" (*The Thirteen Petalled Rose,* p. 46).

The central issue in life is the victory of the soul over itself p. 61

"The point is that God knows the person whom He is testing and is confident that the outcome will be for the good. As a certain Midrash teaches: just as the potter knocks on the newly completed vessel to ascertain if it is sound, so does God knock on a man. A potter will refrain from knocking on an obviously cracked vessel, it would only break; he tests the pots that are whole" (*The Candle of God,* p. 204).

The two souls of man p. 62

In Rabbi Steinsaltz's commentary on the *Tanya,* he writes, "The basis of all that the *Tanya* will say is that every Jew possesses two souls. The existence of these two souls is independent of the person's stature: great and small, righteous and wicked are all equal in this regard. The difference lies in how these souls manifest themselves: which of them finds expression in the person's consciousness and behavior, and on which level and in what manner it does so" (*Opening the Tanya,* p. 56).

The constant struggle between the two souls of man p. 62

"We might say, without going into too much detail, that the world is divided into two 'sides': the side of holiness and the *sitra achra,* which literally means the 'other side.' The side of holiness is the side that relates to the Holy One, encompassing everything that recognizes Him and submits to Him. The other side, as its name implies, has no intrinsic content or identity of its own, being defined solely by the fact that it is not the side of holiness.

"This implies that there is no neutral ground between holiness and unholiness. Every object, force, or phenomenon is either holy or not; if it is not holy, it is of the *sitra achra.* A person who cleaves to God is of the side of holiness; a person who does not cleave to God has placed himself on the other side. One cannot be neutral in his relationship with God: man is either committed to Him and on His side or on the other side" (*Opening the Tanya,* p. 58).

The animal soul as tempter p. 63

See chapter 1 of *The Thirteen Petalled Rose,* in which Rabbi Steinsaltz writes, "Like the angels of holiness, the angels of destruction are, to a degree, channels to transfer the plenty that, as it is transmuted from our world, descends the stairs of corruption, level after level, to the lowest depths of the worlds of abomination. It follows that these worlds of evil act in conjunction with, and directly upon, man, whether in natural, concrete forms or in abstract, spiritual forms. The subversive angels are thus also tempters and insiders to evil, because they bring the knowledge of evil from their world to our world" (p. 20).

Five levels of the soul p. 64

This topic is treated, in its barest essentials, and then only scratching its surface, by Rabbi Steinsaltz in *The Thirteen Petalled Rose.* Chapter 3, "The Soul of Man," is the larger overview of the general subject of the soul. On pages 55–57, Rabbi Steinsaltz outlines the five levels of the soul: *Nefesh, Ruach, Nashamah, Chayah,* and *Yechidah.*

Levels within levels in the soul p. 64

In *The Thirteen Petalled Rose,* Rabbi Steinsaltz speaks of "so many apparently unconnected levels of meaning to each—the levels, moreover appearing to be unconnected—that a mere listing of their names does not adequately convey their essence" (p. 28). Also, Rabbi Steinsaltz warns, "It is not given to transmit something that does not lend itself to material description, and the imagery used is invariably inadequate" (p. 24).

Which soul will rule the other? p. 64

See chapter 9, "The Animal-Soul," in *The Long Shorter Way,* for a thorough treatment of this topic.

Chapter 8: Searching for One's Purpose in Life

A descent for the sake of ascension p. 67

This has always been my favorite paragraph of my favorite book: "The process of soul's connection with the body—called the 'descent of the soul into matter'—is, from a certain perspective, the soul's profound tragedy. But the soul undertakes this terrible risk as a part of the need to descend in order to make the desired ascent to hitherto unknown heights. It is a risk and a danger, because the soul's connection with the body and its contact with the material world where it is the only factor that is free—unbounded by the determinism of physical law and able to choose and move freely—make it possible for the soul to fall and, in falling, to destroy the world. Indeed, Creation itself, and the creation of man, is precisely such a risk, a descent for the sake of ascension" (*The Thirteen Petalled Rose,* p. 39).

Spirituality is not, by definition, holy or glorious p. 68

Rabbi Steinsaltz writes, "Just as there are holy angels, built into and created by the sacred system, there are also destructive angels, called 'devils' or 'demons,' who are the emanations of the connection of man with those aspects of reality which are the opposite of holiness. Here, too, the actions of man and his modes of existence, in all their forms, create angels, but angels of another sort, from another level and a different reality. These are hostile angels that may be part of a lower world or even of a higher or more spiritual world" (*The Thirteen Petalled Rose,* p. 12).

The importance of finding one's purpose p. 69

"It has been said that each of the letters of the Torah has some corresponding soul; that is to say, every soul is a letter in the Torah and has its own part to play" (*The Thirteen Petalled Rose,* p. 47).

Each person has a special gift p. 69

"It is said that in the Torah there are seventy faces, which are the seventy faces of the divine *Shekhinah,* and that these contain six hundred thousand faces in accordance with the number of primary souls of Israel, so that every individual soul has a certain part in the Torah" (*The Thirteen Petalled Rose,* p. 76).

The soul may repeat a lifetime p. 70

Rabbi Steinsaltz discusses the topic in *The Thirteen Petalled Rose*. "It has been said that each of the letters of the Torah has some corresponding soul; that is to say, every soul is a letter in the entire Torah and has its own part to play. The soul that has fulfilled its task, that has done what it has to do in terms of creating or repairing its own part of the world and realizing its own essence, can wait after death for the perfection of the world as a whole. But not all the souls are so privileged: many stray for one reason or another; sometimes a person does not do all the proper things, and sometimes he misuses forces and spoils his portion and the portion of others. In such cases the soul does not complete its task and may even itself be damaged by contact with the world. It has not managed to complete that portion of reality which only this particular soul can complete; and therefore after the death of the body, the soul returns and is reincarnated in the body of another person and again must try and complete what it failed to correct or what it injured in the past. The sins of man are not eliminated so long as this soul does not complete that which it has to complete. From which it may be seen that most souls are not new, they are not in the world for the first time. Almost every person bears the legacy of previous existences. Generally, one does not obtain the previous self again, for the soul manifests itself in different circumstances and in different situations. What is more, some souls are compounded of more than one single former person and shares parts of a number of persons" (p. 47).

Rabbi Steinsaltz makes it clear that reincarnation is an accepted part of Jewish theology as expressed by many leading sages. The soul's task is to raise its consciousness. "Consciousness, assuming ever renewed identification along the lifeline of the soul, is the way of man's ascent to perfection" (*The Thirteen Petalled Rose*, p. 43).

The souls of two people can grow into a genuine unity p. 71

"The unattached individual is not yet a whole person; the whole individual is always double, man and woman" (*The Thirteen Petalled Rose,* p. 124).

The greatest happiness is the pleasure of being alive p. 71

The subject of this pebble is explored in Part V of this book.

There is a path that leads upward p. 72

"This level of the perfection of all humanity, in which a new relation will exist between body and soul, and the world will be whole with itself, is called 'Heaven' or the 'next world.' It is the goal toward which all the souls of men, in discharging their private and specific tasks in life, aspire and strive" (*The Thirteen Petalled Rose,* p. 49).

Becoming absorbed in the task of Divine work p. 72

See Rabbi Steinsaltz's essay "Soul-Searching" in *The Strife of the Spirit* for a lengthy exploration of related themes.

The person who has not found God has not labored hard or long enough p. 73

In *The Thirteen Petalled Rose,* Rabbi Steinsaltz writes, "It takes both time and considerable introspection to get beyond the elaborate mental constructions, the words and ideas, devised by everyone" (p. 104). And "It is . . . a continuous going, a going after God, a going to God, day after day, year after year" (p. 99).

Why children are often wise p. 74

As we know, Moses was the most humble person, and humility is a deeply important trait. Rabbi Steinsaltz writes, "A person must do more than act humbly. He must posses an internal, intrinsic sense of humility" (*Understanding the Tanya,* p. 76).

What is life? What is it all for? p. 74

For an essay by Rabbi Steinsaltz on the book of Ecclesiastes, see the essay "Ecclesiastes" in *On Being Free.*

The special key to the private door p. 75

"Every person has his own spiritual essence whose uniqueness not only is the result of his heredity and education but exists by divine intention. For each and every human being has a specific task to perform in the world, a task that no one else can accomplish" (*The Thirteen Petalled Rose,* p. 75).

Chapter 9: Spiritual Progress

The spiritual life has become dominated by a shallow standard of measure p. 77

A further indication of the limitations of psychology: "Even though the question of the self is one that has since the beginning of time been contemplated by many profound minds, it is not really a philosophical problem. Philosophical, psychological, or scientific treatment of it only provides different frameworks and forms of expression for answers that are in any case continuously being proven inadequate" (*The Thirteen Petalled Rose,* p. 104).

All calculations of who is a saint and who is a sinner belong to God p. 77

Further exploration of related themes by Rabbi Steinsaltz can be found in the chapter "The Wicked Man Who Prospers" in *The Long Shorter Way.*

The ability to see depends on one's purity of heart p. 78

Important remarks by Rabbi Steinsaltz about the Holy Land are in the chapter "Holiness" in *The Thirteen Petalled Rose:* "The holiness of the Holy Land has nothing to do with who the inhabitants are or what they do; it is a choice from on high, beyond human comprehension" (p. 53).

Our vision is limited to a narrow range p. 79

"We know that human vision assimilates only a small fragment of the spectrum; as far as our senses are concerned, the rest of it does not exist" (*The Thirteen Petalled Rose,* p. 8).

The aspiration to perfect the soul and elevate the world p. 79

"The soul that has fulfilled its task, that has done what it has to do in terms of creating or repairing its own part of the world and realizing its own essence, can wait after death for the perfection of the world as a whole" (*The Thirteen Petalled Rose,* p. 47).

The same place can be holy to one person and commonplace to another p. 81

"Each soul understands and does things in a way not suitable for another soul" (*The Thirteen Petalled Rose,* p. 76).

The festivals are internal events in the life of the individual p. 82

"In order for a person to gain the benefit of this special day, he must concentrate his energies and focus his consciousness on this significant idea and its symbolic representations; he has to tune himself to catch its resonance. The numerous and various details of the Commandments then cease to be burdensome and are accepted wholly as an outer expression, the clear and specified relationship of the person with the fundamental spiritual experience" (*The Thirteen Petalled Rose,* p. 121). Also, "these holy festivals are not intended simply as memorial days to keep alive the memory of the events; they are divinely appointed times dedicated to a renewal of the same revelation that once occurred on that day in the year, a repetition and a restoration of the same forces. So . . . the sanctity of the holidays is derived not only from a primal divine revelation but also from Israel's continual resanctification, in the way it keeps these days holy, of this revelation" (p. 58).

One should compare people on the basis of their efforts p. 82

"Everyone can and should learn from others the proper way of doing things, but in the end each person has to follow his own winding path to the goal that is his heart's desire. Some lives have an emotional emphasis; others, an intellectual; for some the way of joy is natural; for others existence is full of effort and struggle; there are people for whom purity of heart is the most difficult thing in the world, while for others it is given as a gift from birth" (*The Thirteen Petalled Rose,* p. 76).

What a child learns has to be correct p. 83

As recorded in *On the Road with Rabbi Steinsaltz,* "Rabbi Steinsaltz said to me, 'Don't teach your children the things that ultimately they're going to have to overcome. If you teach your children that God is an old man with a long beard who lives in the sky, then when that child gets older, it will be even more difficult to come close to God because before any progress can be made, first an old image has to be discarded. Always aim for the highest expression of the truth with your children'" (pp. 64–65).

The capacity for self-deception is enormous p. 83

For a discussion of this self-deception, see *Understanding the Tanya:* "Dullness is an impure sheath covering a person's heart. It is made of self-satisfaction and an egotistical sense of being" (p. 57).

Moving but staying in the same place p. 84

Rabbi Steinsaltz writes, "To remain in any one condition of being, above or below, represents a cessation of effort, a dying, and therefore an evil" (*The Thirteen Petalled Rose,* p. 79).

What will I get out of the next life? p. 85

See all the pebbles in Chapter Ten of this book, "Repentence." "For every wrong deed in his past, the penitent is required to perform certain acts that surpass what is demanded of an 'ordinary' individual, to complement and balance the picture of his life. He must build and create anew and change the order of good and evil in such a way that not only his current life activity acquires new form and direction, but the totality of his life receives a consistently positive value" (*The Thirteen Petalled Rose,* p. 101).

Chapter 10: Repentance

Repentance is a total upheaval p. 87

"A person has to undergo a transformation so drastic that his entire being, and all his deeds and thoughts, acquire a new and different significance. In effect, he passes into a new field of reality, where everything is completely different from what it was" (*Opening the Tanya,* p. 192).

The shock of *teshuvah* p. 88

During a lecture given in New York City, Rabbi Steinsaltz said, "I grew up in a family where neither my mother nor my father went to synagogue. Not even on Yom Kippur. My father said that he did not go because he had too much respect for the place. He said that the synagogue is not a theater. Either you are a participant, or you don't go there. Because he could not be a participant, he would not go to watch.

"My father was not particular about eating kosher when he was in Israel. But whenever he was abroad, he always ate kosher just for everyone to see. He was proud of being a Jew and of Jewish knowledge. When I was ten years old, my father hired a tutor to teach me Talmud. My father said, 'I don't mind if you're an atheist, but I don't want any member of my family to be an ignoramus.'

"It is a shame for a Jew to be an ignoramus. Perhaps it is the lowest of the low that a Jew can reach. It means he lacks some essential knowledge about himself. Imagine that a person does not know that he has a head until he is sixty-five and that he discovered it accidentally. That is the kind of feeling that results from a Jew being ignorant."

The chart of human progress is not simple p. 88

"When a person turns his back on someone, he might be in close proximity to that person—they might even be pressed against each other back to back—yet they are as far apart from each other as they can possibly be. *Teshuvah,* then, is a shift in the orientation: a person turning to God, after having spurned Him" (*Opening the Tanya,* pp. 90–91).

Knowledge of one's sins can result in a transformation p. 89

"The act of repentance is, in the first place, a severance of the chain of cause and effect in which one transgression follows inevitably upon another. Beyond this, it is an attempt to nullify and even alter the past. This can be achieved only when man, subjectively, shatters the order of his own existence" (*The Thirteen Petalled Rose,* p. 100).

Three stages of spiritual development p. 90

"A person who is in a state of repentance throughout his life is not someone who must atone for a particular sin but someone who is returning to God, to the source and root of his soul, coming ever closer and growing ever more intimately connected to Him, walking upon the path that reaches to infinity, a path without end on which one walks forever, in this state of repentance throughout one's life" (*Understanding the Tanya,* p. 107).

Transforming one's sinful deeds into something meritorious p. 91

"The highest level of repentance, however, lies beyond the correction of sinful deeds and the creation of independent, new patterns that counterweigh past sins and injuries; it is reached when the change and the correction penetrate the very essence of the sins once committed and, as the sages say, create the condition in which a man's transgressions become his merits" (*The Thirteen Petalled Rose,* p. 101).

Our goal is always to aim for greater heights p. 91

"True *teshuvah* is when a person craves to return to God with the same intensity, with the same turmoil, as the craving he experienced at the time of his sin. The sin does not then become a *mitzvah,* but the *teshuvah* redirects it to function as a *mitzvah* does, as an impetus of bringing a person closer to God" (*Opening the Tanya,* p. 195).

One's life as an annex of the Holy Temple p. 93

"The Holy of Holies is made manifest only when everything is as it should be, when the Temple stands at its appointed location, and when everything in the Temple is so perfectly ordered and arranged that it is pervaded by the *Shekhinah*" (*The Thirteen Petalled Rose,* p. 52).

The chief work of man is to make corrections p. 93

"The literal meaning of 'repentance,' *teshuvah,* is 'return'—the return of the divine soul to its source, which is also the source and root of all worlds" (*Understanding the Tanya,* p. 106).

Using a certain skill of a wrestler p. 94

"The penitent . . . must break free of the chains, the limitations, and the restrictions imposed by environment and education" (*The Thirteen Petalled Rose,* p. 95).

The effort one makes to break free of the past is also a part of the effort to find one's true self. As Rabbi Steinsaltz writes, "In spite of the vast range of ways in which a Jew can alienate himself from his past and express himself in foreign cultural forms, he nevertheless retains a metaphysically, almost genetically, imprinted image of his Jewishness. To use a metaphor from the world of botany: a change of climate, soil, or other physical conditions can induce marked alterations in the form and the functioning of a plant, and even the adoption of characteristics of other species and genera, but the unique paradigm or prototype persists" (*The Thirteen Petalled Rose,* p. 95).

In Judaism, children were never considered little angels p. 95

In his book *We Jews,* Rabbi Steinsaltz offers an interesting and provocative discussion about children. Although children were never considered little angels, Rabbi Steinsaltz writes, "The adult can measure his limitations and assess what he is capable of, and, even more so, what he is totally incapable of doing. However, such barriers do not exist for the child, and certainly cannot stand in the way of his dreams. Since he has no idea of his human and personal limitations, there is nothing to prevent him from planning, dreaming, and wanting things that perhaps can never be actually realized. Therefore, the Jewish child dreams the messianic dream" (p. 101).

Walking the path to infinity p. 95

"So one who undergoes such a *teshuvah* has his sins transformed into merits. The very sin he committed, his very disconnection and alienation from God, is what now fuels his greater and more intense love of God" (*Opening the Tanya,* p. 194).

We do *teshuvah* in a universe that transcends physical laws p. 96

"The essence of repentance is not a specific action. It is not a recipe that one follows: so much charity, so many self afflictions, so many fasts. Essentially, repentance is a feeling of the heart—regret over the past and a resolution for the future.

"The greater the depths of a person's mind and the development of his maturity, the more clearly he can recognize his problems and the more profoundly he can see each flaw. And then his previous repentance may no longer seem to be enough, for he looks downward to levels of imperfection that his previous repentance had not been able to reach" (*Understanding the Tanya,* pp. 51–52).

It's easy to fool oneself p. 97

"Our sages say, 'A person only sins when a spirit of insanity enters him.' The *baal teshuvah* ('penitent') is one who cures himself of this insanity, who now realizes that he performed his previous actions without a true understanding and awareness of their significance. With such repentance, he severs himself from his past and attains new perspective on himself and his life, on his past and his future" (*Opening the Tanya,* p. 191).

Chapter 11: The Pursuit of Happiness

The quest is not for peace of mind p. 99

"Indeed, man's question should not be how to escape the perpetual struggle but rather what form to give it, at what level to wage it" (*The Strife of the Spirit,* p. 8).

Great happiness is not the goal of life p. 99

"The notion of peace of mind as a supreme value, as a standard by which to judge all other aspects of life, is worse than inadequate. It carries with it the real danger of apotheosizing emptiness and negation—negation of good as well as evil, release from achievement as well as from stress" (*The Strife of the Spirit,* p. 5).

To be truly free p. 100

"Attaining freedom by accepting the yoke of the kingdom of heaven is not a simple or self-evident thing" (*On Being Free,* p. 29).

Spiritually free p. 101

Highly recommended are the essays by Rabbi Steinsaltz in *On Being Free* directly related to the subject of freedom.

The elementary meaning of freedom p. 102

There are a number of essays by Rabbi Steinsaltz on themes related to freedom and slavery on the Aleph Society's Web site, http://www.steinsaltz.org.

To be free means to have a life goal of one's own p. 103

Rabbi Steinsaltz, an animal lover and former member of the board of the Jerusalem Zoo, in conversation with a journalist said, "I have had my own experience with zoology, and I remember once seeing something that made a big impression on me. It was a plucked peacock. When you see a plucked peacock, which looks like a rather ugly, emaciated hen, you get so very disappointed because when you see the peacock in all its glory, it's clearly a glorious bird. But again, if you want to eat it or have more contact, then you find out what it is in truth. So when I see peacock feathers, which are wonderful to look at, I always think about the plucked bird beneath those feathers."

PART III: THE CHILDREN OF ISRAEL
Chapter 12: What Does It Mean to Be Jewish?

The Jews, as a people, are obsessed with God p. 107

In *The Thirteen Petalled Rose,* Rabbi Steinsaltz refers to our "desire to approach God" (p. 96). It is our desire whether we know it or not.

The uniting element is undeniably there p. 108

Rabbi Steinsaltz writes, "The basic feeling that Judaism is a family connection also works upward, in terms of a parent-child relation to God, with the national-religious essence felt as an inner family relation that is not the province of abstract theology or political definition. It is no less so in the horizontal connection within the Jewish community, which remains that of the members of the family.

"This basic feeling explains, on the one hand, the great intimacy of the Jewish tie, the very real feeling of brotherhood between Jews even when they have nothing much in common. That which is written, 'we are brothers, sons of the one man' (Genesis 42:12), has been used by Jews of all generations in all lands, in spite of huge differences between them. It expresses the blood kinship of a brotherhood that goes beyond space and familiarity and common destiny" (*We Jews,* pp. 56–57).

Defining a Jewish community p. 109

"A Jew is inwardly compelled to come to the defense of a fellow Jew by a family feeling that may be well hidden from his own awareness" (*We Jews,* p. 58).

We Jews are optimists p. 109

As a point of interest, Rabbi Steinsaltz shares another teaching from Rabbi Chaim Vital in *Opening the Tanya:*

"The concept of a good inclination and evil inclination in the heart of man abounds in the Talmud and the Midrashim. What is unique about Rabbi Chaim Vital's statement is that he speaks of two souls, two entire personas, each with a full set of intellectual and emotional faculties and inclinations . . . [which] are actually the traits, drives, and desires of their respective souls" (pp. 56–57).

A real Jew would rather die than worship idols p. 110

Similarly, Rabbi Steinsaltz writes, "This profound sense of kinship may also explain the dramatically unpredictable responses of many persons who all their lives were far removed from anything Jewish, and yet when pressed by outer forces to forgo this connection with Jewishness, refused, and were prepared to pay the utmost penalty. The list of Jewish martyrs throughout the ages includes not only Saints who sacrificed their lives for God, but also people of much lesser stature, individuals who were far removed from religion or Jewish consciousness" (*We Jews,* p. 58).

Rabbi Steinsaltz also explores this subject in his essay "The Test of Jewishness" in *The Strife of the Spirit.*

What is it that we are so eager to pass on? p. 111

Recommended exploration of this subject by Rabbi Steinsaltz can be found is his essay "Heritage and Inheritance," remarks delivered at the annual Aleph Society dinner in Jerusalem on September 25, 1996. This can be found at http://www.steinsaltz.org.

The Jews are a stiff-necked people p. 112

At the end of each chapter of *We Jews,* I was given the opportunity to present Rabbi Steinsaltz with questions. When asked about the character trait of persistence, Rabbi Steinsaltz said, "Persistence and obstinacy are enormously important, and Jews have been known, and are alternately proud and not proud, for being hard-headed and unable to move. Determining which things are important and which are not is the essence of life. They may be your family, your environment, your chosen way of life. The ability to be persistent and to go on and not allow yourself to be diverted is important here. On the other hand, if a person becomes obstinate about any kind of little thing, then it is basically damaging. So I have to decide that I will be obstinate only about important things" (p. 78).

Being Jewish means we have obligations p. 113

"Nations that are considered barbaric, of an inferior level, and degenerate are described or treated favorably whenever they show some progressive trait that others do not expect to find in them. Among such people, any good action will simply be considered noble, any action that is not completely base will be considered a good deed, and any activity that elsewhere would be normal is considered progressive and viewed as some special advance.

"As we have said, the very opposite is true for those who have any sense of being chosen. For them, every descent is a double degradation, every defect stands out and is recognizable to all, and no action that is excused in others is forgiven in them. This double standard is practiced, of course, in the attitude toward the state of Israel. This state is criticized and accused for every deed that is normally condoned in other states" (*We Jews,* p. 173).

The concept of Israel means me p. 114

As readers can plainly see, many subjects and themes in this section of pebbles is treated at greater length in Rabbi Steinsaltz's book *We Jews,* including this: "The connection of a Jew to his people is not dependent on his being in any particular place or on some religious or cultural tie" (pp. 48–49).

The only way we can really know ourselves p. 114

As Rabbi Steinsaltz writes, "If pursued aimlessly, with no clear goal, this primal search does not transcend the urge to be free; without a vector, it can be spiritually exhausting and may never lead to a genuine discovery of the true self. In this respect, not in vain has the Torah been perceived as a system of knowledge and insights that guide the individual Jew to reach his own pattern of selfhood. The mutual relationship between the individual Jew and Judaism, between the man and his God, depends on the fact that Judaism is not only the Law, the prescribed religious practice, but [also] a life framework that embraces his entire existence; furthermore, it is ultimately the only framework in which, in his aloneness and in his search, he will be able to find himself. Whereas potentially a man can adapt himself, there exists, whether he acknowledges it or not, a path that is his own, which relates to him, to his family, to his home" (*The Thirteen Petalled Rose,* p. 95).

Chapter 13: The Jewish Family

We are a family p. 117

This subject is explored in some detail in "Are We a Nation or a Religion?"—chapter 3 of Rabbi Steinsaltz's book *We Jews.* As a point of interest, the majority of the book was written by Rabbi Steinsaltz in 1990 while he was scholar in residence at the Woodrow Wilson International Center for Scholars in Washington, D.C., which serves as a think tank for the United States Congress and executive branch.

We are not a perfect family, but we are a real family p. 118

In "Do We Have Our Own Set of Character Traits?"—chapter 4 of *We Jews*—Rabbi Steinsaltz offers a fascinating discussion about the double-sided nature of some Jewish character traits. See "Our qualities, like all qualities, are double-sided" (pp. 75–76).

The connection is beyond choice p. 119

Although Judaism does not proselytize, the Jewish people do welcome converts. In *We Jews,* Rabbi Steinsaltz says, while exploring the phenomenon of conversion to Judaism, "There is also the notion that when, as it is said, the Almighty offered the Torah to the nations and only the Children of Israel accepted it, there must have been some members of the other nations ready to accept the Torah. Converts may be the souls of those people who were ready to accept the Torah. But when you deal with it in a more concrete way, it is not mystical; basically it is a ceremony of adoption. The convert is getting into the family, not only getting into the religion. Nobody can get into the Jewish religion without getting into the family, so it's an adoption" (pp. 59–60).

Finding out to which family one belongs p. 119

"In spite of the vast range of ways in which a Jew can alienate himself from his past and express himself in foreign cultural forms, he nevertheless retains a metaphysically, almost genetically, imprinted image of his Jewishness" (*The Thirteen Petalled Rose,* p. 95).

Judaism is the way we as a family move p. 120

In *On the Road with Rabbi Steinsaltz,* a conversation with Rabbi Steinsaltz is described as follows: "He told me that he was once invited by the BBC to participate in a documentary about the world's religions and that he was asked to represent Judaism—and they gave him one minute.

"He told me that he said, 'What can I say? I can say that Jews believe in God. But other religions believe in God. I can say that Jews believe in revelation. But other religions believe in revelation. I can say all kinds of things that Jews do, but other religions do these things too. I suppose all I can really say is that we Jews do it in a Jewish way' " (p. 33).

The truth of being home p. 121

Rabbi Steinsaltz writes, "Whereas potentially a man can adapt himself, there exists, whether he acknowledges it or not, a path that is his own, which relates to him, to his family, to his home" (*The Thirteen Petalled Rose,* p. 96).

Israel is an entity p. 121

"Jews are like the limbs of a single body. We might think of it as an organic entity, which is more than a collection of its parts. We would not consider 600 chairs as an organic entity, but the 613 limbs of the body and the 613 *mitzvot* are" (*Understanding the Tanya,* p. 123).

The definition of a Jew is beyond biology p. 122

In a section called "A 'Holy Nation' Includes Everybody" in *We Jews,* Rabbi Steinsaltz writes, "The existence of a 'holy nation' means that this role of world priesthood is not the role of a particular people within the nation, but of the entire Jewish people, with all its members great and small" (p. 147).

O Guardian of Israel, protect the remnant of Israel p. 123

This excerpt of a talk given by Rabbi Steinsaltz was published in a wonderful collection of essays gathered by Thomas Nisell, a close colleague of the Rabbi's. The essay, titled "The Time Is Short and the Work Is Great," appears in the book *A Dear Son to Me* (see Bibliography).

Chapter 14: The Jewish Family in Jeopardy

We are bleeding with smiles on our faces p. 125

"The inescapable conclusion is that, at least in the Diaspora, the Jewish people are in a demographic decline. We are shrinking and becoming older. If nothing dramatic occurs to reverse these trends, it may be that the Jewish community should no longer concern itself with building schools, but with constructing more old-age homes and larger cemeteries" (from a syndicated column titled "Jewish Demography: An Alarming Trend," available at http://www.steinsaltz.org).

We will need a memorial for the Jews we lose through assimilation p. 126

Also from "Jewish Demography: An Alarming Trend": "The recent survey of American Jewry—at least the parts that have been released thus far—contains demographic data that should alarm anyone who has an interest in the continuity of the Jewish people.

"The data describe a community that is slowly, but inexorably, dying out."

Jewish education is so lacking that it almost has no meaning p. 126

"From Childhood to Old Age" is an essay on the "inner aspect of education." It is available at http://www.steinsaltz.org and would be of profound interest to the reader interested in education.

Kosher-centered Judaism p. 127

Careful performance of the Divine commandments—the positive *mitzvot* and the prohibitions, transmitted through the written Torah and oral tradition—is considered essential in Jewish spiritual practice.

That being said, an anecdote that has circulated widely for years, retold in my book *On the Road with Rabbi Steinsaltz,* is, unfortunately, often misunderstood.

Here is the anecdote: "Rabbi Steinsaltz had been teaching a weekly Talmud class for a number of years that was attended by secular academics. At one point, a filmmaker approached the Rabbi and expressed interest in joining the class. But he said, 'Rabbi, I want you to know that I eat bacon every Shabbos.'

" 'Every Shabbos?' Rabbi Steinsaltz asked.

" 'Yes, every Shabbos,' the professor replied.

"So Rabbi Steinsaltz said, 'Why every Shabbos?'

"And the filmmaker said, 'I have a busy week. Most days I barely have time for a cup of coffee. But then the weekend comes, and I fix myself a great breakfast—and I include bacon every time.'

"Rabbi Steinsaltz responded, 'It says in the Torah that we should honor Shabbos. It's surely not my way, but I suppose it has some merit to honor Shabbos with bacon than not to honor Shabbos at all' " (pp. 196–197).

The point of the story is not that it is OK to eat bacon, which is forbidden by Jewish law, but rather that one can—and perhaps should—attempt to extract something positive from a negative situation.

Too long, too boring, and too frequent p. 127

Anyone who participates in reciting the kiddush ritual on Friday evening would be enriched by reading Rabbi Steinsaltz's essay "An Additional Note on the Kiddush Ritual," which is the last chapter of the original edition of *The Thirteen Petalled Rose*.

Jewish leaders don't even understand Jewish jokes p. 128

The book *We Jews* ends on a hopeful note. Rabbi Steinsaltz writes, "There are still enough Jews here. Many of them, even though very estranged from anything Jewish, are nonetheless good people. We have here, all in all, a fair number of individuals who are first-rate. These people can become the foundation for a different, better future.

"But we cannot expect this building to construct itself. There can be hope in our future, a promise, something to reach for. If we want to have such tomorrow—a real tomorrow, and not just a bleak putting off of death for another half generation—it will require a great deal of effort. But although this work is unprecedented, it can be done" (pp. 187–188).

The Jewish people must regain its own essence p. 129

"The prophets protested against the preoccupation with sacrifices even in the Temple, as opposed to inward religious commitment, not because they were opposed to the sacrifices, but because this worship became more and more a focal point in itself.

"They detach one from the perception of divinity and become a relationship to something materialistic—even though they be holy—and they become more and more detached from inward devotion.

"The evil inclination of idolatry is the outcome of a conflict between the deep need for religion, faith, and serving God, and the human difficulty of creating a relationship with an abstraction. This conflict, this tension, is what creates the temptation to satisfy the longing for the divine with something perverse—that is, by means of idolatry, cultic ritual, and devotion to something simpler and easier for human beings.

"It is thus that the urge toward faith takes the form of idolatry. Sometimes when a person finds that the existing forms do not suit him any longer, the urge is to create a new god, a new faith.

"The Midrash has already said that quite often, when a Gentile sees a new type of god that he has never seen before, he says, 'This is a Jewish god.'

"That is to say, [he sees] another god that the Jews have created for themselves in order to satisfy their desire and inclination to serve them" (*We Jews,* p. 136).

The destruction of the Holy Temple is a key to all of Israel's troubles p. 130

"Though the potential for holiness persists forever, it is true that the holiness of the Land of Israel cannot be adequately manifested unless all the constituents of the circles of sanctity radiating from the center in Jerusalem are in their proper places. Thus, when the Temple is not standing, all the aspects of holiness that grow out of it become vague and uncertain, some of them sinking into a state of only latent sanctity, indicating no more than a possibility and a starting point" (*The Thirteen Petalled Rose,* p. 53).

When we are not one, Israel is in a state of deprivation and suffering p. 131

"Whenever there is a threat from outside, the Jewish family reacts as a united body. It is not necessarily a rational response to attack. Often it would be more convenient and logical for an individual Jew or the people as a whole to pay no attention to a Jewish troublemaker. But that is simply not done. There is no clear reasoning involved. A Jew is inwardly compelled to come to the defense of a fellow Jew by a family feeling that may be well hidden from his own awareness" (*We Jews,* p. 58).

The destiny of the Jewish person who has been estranged p. 132

"Jews in the Diaspora have only two choices. Either they can give up, close shop, and say, 'We are defeated,' or they can create a new way, a new hope. If people want to go on, if they have a feeling that there is something in it, if the memory of the half-obliterated document still possesses some compelling power, then the Jewish life in [the United States] must be rebuilt. Let me say something full of chutzpah: there is a need for, a use for, and even a possibility of making this place something like *Galut Bavel,* the ancient Jewish place of exile in Babylonia. It is possible to create a second center, comparable to, possibly better than, the main center in Israel. But to accomplish this, one has to do much more than survive. If you cannot do it right, if you cannot create something that will be worthwhile spiritually and intellectually, it is not worth doing at all" (*We Jews,* pp. 186–187).

A symptom of the spiritual malady from which we are suffering p. 133

"In the large scheme of history it may be observed that the Jewish people, who grew up and reached a certain maturity in its own land, was in exile for hundreds of years. This meant the loss of much more than national sovereignty. Whole areas of tradition were abandoned and only vague hints survived in memory. One can hardly reconstruct the richness of this tradition from the written evidence.

"To a degree, the Temple, the legal and social structure, the schools and synagogues can be pieced together in some fashion or other. The mystical traditions are far more elusive to the modern researcher. Most of them have been totally wiped out by time, such as the schools of the prophets. We have nothing resembling such schools, either in Israel or in the Diaspora.

"In fact, there have been attempts to make such a restoration by pasting scattered indications together. Some of this material has survived only in written form; most of it is considered irretrievably lost.

"Nevertheless, the dream or hope or restitution has remained. In the days to come, a regeneration is possible, if the right stimulant appears. This anticipation is possible because, as in every organic entity, the code of the whole is contained in the fragments, so that from the little that has come down to us it may be possible to reconstruct a semblance of the ancient tradition" (*On Being Free,* pp. 230–231).

Life is not a vicarious activity p. 133

"It may be that a specific person, many people, and even the greater part of the nation will try to escape from its inner essence, to deny it, or to exchange it—entirely or partially—for other purposes and values. Yet every such attempt at escape and denial, even if it actually succeeds, is a failure from the inner viewpoint. It is a denial not only of the past, of the heritage, or the national duty, however confused it may be, but an escape from the person's essential nature. The changes that are made by everyone are merely masks, disguises, imitations—the exchange of the essential me for other identities. This escape may be successful externally, but it is really a kind of suicide, a denial of the main essence, an escape from the true self" (*We Jews,* p. 152).

A blessing or a curse? p. 134

"But is it not possible for someone to return who was never 'there,' who has no memories of a Jewish way of life, for whom Judaism is not a personal but a historical or biological heritage, or no more than an epithet that gives him a certain meaningless identity? The answer is unequivocally in the affirmative, for—on the more profound level—repentance as return reaches beyond such personal configurations. It is indeed a return to Judaism, but not to the external framework, not to the religious norms that man seeks to understand or to integrate into, with their clear-cut formulae, directives, actions, rituals; it is a return to one's own paradigm, to the prototype of the Jewish person" (*The Thirteen Petalled Rose,* p. 94).

PART IV: TORAH

Chapter 15: The Nature of Torah

The Torah comes to man across the abyss of the infinite p. 137

Chapter Two of this book gathers pebbles about the Infinite, blessed be He. And many other pebbles can be found throughout this book focusing on some aspect of grasping the

Infinite. We try constantly to reject old models of the Infinite and push our attempts at definitions to expand even further. In chapter 2 of *The Thirteen Petalled Rose,* Rabbi Steinsaltz writes about it and concludes, "When we speak of the Infinite, Blessed be He, we mean the utmost of perfection and abstraction, that which encompasses everything and is beyond all possible limits" (p. 25).

There are many ways to connect with the Torah p. 138

An important thread running throughout Rabbi Steinsaltz's teachings and these pebbles is acknowledgment of the unique path of each individual. *Parabola* magazine explores this understanding with Rabbi Steinsaltz in an interview, reprinted in *The Strife of the Spirit,* titled "The Private Gate." Rabbi Steinsaltz says, "We believe that the Law has at least 600,000 different paths within it for individuals to enter. There is what is called 'the private gate' for each of us. And we each have to find our own gate. The search for my own particular gate can be a very arduous one. A man may search for years and find only doorways that are not his; he may go on through all his life without really finding it" (p. 225).

The Torah is like a tale within a tale within a tale p. 139

Rabbi Steinsaltz also uses the word "tale" in *The Thirteen Petalled Rose*. Regarding what he calls the question of the self and the search for oneself ("Who am I?"), Rabbi Steinsaltz writes, "The question appears in the very first story of the Bible—the story of Adam and Eve. . . . This question, like the entire *tale* . . ." (p. 105). The Torah is not fiction; nor is it nonfiction. It is more true than nonfiction, "a tale within a tale within a tale."

The Torah is always expanding p. 140

In the final paragraph of the last chapter of Rabbi Steinsaltz's book *The Essential Talmud,* he writes, "The work, a compilation of the endeavors of many generations that is edited with excessive precision and has been studied by tens of thousands of scholars, still remains a challenge. Of the verse, 'I have seen an end of every purpose,' the sages said: 'Everything has its boundaries, even Heaven and earth have their boundaries. Only Torah has no bounds'" (p. 303).

The Torah descends so it can be grasped by mortals p. 140

Rabbi Steinsaltz, in *The Thirteen Petalled Rose,* writes, "One who is immersed in Torah becomes a partner with God, in the sense that man on one hand and God on the other are participating in the planning, the spinning out of the idea, the common dream of the existence of the world" (p. 66).

Relating to the Torah for its own sake p. 142

In the chapter "Elixir of Death" in his book *In the Beginning,* Rabbi Steinsaltz writes, "The sages have been well aware of the many sides of Torah. Whether it is an elixir of life or an elixir of death depends on whether the person who occupies himself with it is pure in heart and is open to receive what it confers" (p. 201).

Later in the chapter, Rabbi Steinsaltz writes, "How does the elixir of death operate? It does not occur when someone makes an error in Torah; it happens when a person tries to fix it up or when he finds all sorts of wonderful things in it and makes them his own. Gradually the book becomes adjusted to him, becoming *his* Torah" (p. 206).

The Torah's awesome power p. 142

"As someone aptly summed it up: other religions have a concept of scripture as deriving *from* Heaven, but only Judaism seems to be based on the idea that Torah Scripture *is itself* Heaven" (*The Thirteen Petalled Rose,* p. 65).

Chapter 16: Torah Study

The study of Torah is weighed against all the commandments p. 145

"As the sages have said: before Creation, God looked into the Torah and made the world accordingly. By which it is implied that the Torah is the original pattern, or inner plan, of the world" (*The Thirteen Petalled Rose,* p. 65).

It doesn't matter on what level one studies p. 146

Rabbi Steinsaltz writes in the essay "Talmud Torah" in his book *Teshuvah,* "Torah-study is not just a way of gaining entrée to the other *mitzvot,* but a fundamental *mitzvah* in its own right, incumbent on every Jew as long as he lives. One must not rest content with 'pious ignorance,' but rather strive for real achievement in the realm of Jewish learning, in all its branches" (p. 94).

All the levels are revealed p. 146

See the pebbles in Chapter Eighteen, "Kabbalah." Rabbi Steinsaltz makes the point that Kabbalah and Talmud, for example, are two different languages that say the same thing.

When a person studies Torah, he creates an angel p. 146

In "Worlds," the first chapter of *The Thirteen Petalled Rose,* angels are discussed. (A second, slightly different, and always illuminating version can be found in *The Strife of the Spirit* under the title "Worlds, Angels, and Men.") Rabbi Steinsaltz writes, "The angel cannot reveal its true form to man, whose being, senses, and instruments of perception belong only to the world of action: in the world of action there are no means of grasping the angel. It continues to belong to a different dimension even when apprehended in one form or another. This may be compared with those frequencies of electromagnetic fields that are beyond the limited range ordinarily perceived by our senses. We know that human vision assimilates only a small fragment of the spectrum; as far as our senses are concerned, the rest of it does not exist" (*The Thirteen Petalled Rose,* p. 8).

Being trapped by the metaphor p. 147

One of the most illuminating essays by Rabbi Steinsaltz is called "The Imagery Concept in Jewish Thought" and can be found in *The Strife of the Spirit.* Rabbi Steinsaltz concludes, "By aspiring to deeper comprehension, by trying to apprehend the basic ideas and not just the irrelevant appendages of the imagery, we shall be able to observe that the source books of Jewish thought are—with all their so-called outmoded ideas and images—new and vitally meaningful" (p. 70).

If Torah study is not for the sake of Heaven, it is no more than playing p. 148

Rabbi Steinsaltz writes, "Let us take as an illustration the case of a man studying Torah. He becomes elated at having found something new and interesting, a *chidush,* an innovation. And indeed the Torah may very well have revealed something marvelous to him and his joy may be a genuine intellectual elation unrelated to his ego. Or it may be a feeling of exultation at having gotten the better of someone else, of showing himself to be more clever, more successful than others. That is to say, it can be a joy of spiritual experience or it can be a joy of the shell. This person can continue to study Torah and keep enjoying the occupation with Holy Scripture while all the time being involved in idolatrous worship of himself. He can even be immersed in Torah in order to maintain a barrier between himself and people, because he dislikes people. Perhaps the more he shrinks from the people around him, the more intensely he will bury himself in study. Hatred of others can hardly be considered a basis for love of God and His Torah" (*In the Beginning,* p. 218).

The proper relation to Scripture p. 149

Rabbi Steinsaltz writes, "[The] Torah is not merely words of wisdom. It is beyond all wisdom; it is God's wisdom, and the *mitzvot* are God's commandments. The essence of the Torah is that the Creator of the world communicates to man something that man can hear, comprehend, and do and thereby connect with Him. The essence of the connection is created not by the fact that a certain person studies a lot, prays excessively, or observes the *mitzvot* with great zeal but by the very fact that one is doing what God wants one to do" (*Opening the Tanya,* p. 123).

Each of us has the ability to "channel" God p. 150

"The person really listening to the question, or to life's echo of it, may, in his attentiveness and in his reflection on what he hears, be able to discern not only the elemental issue but even the voice of the one asking the question" (*The Thirteen Petalled Rose,* p. 106).

Participating in the Divine planning process p. 152

"When a person performs a commandment, the limbs of his body become a vehicle for the divine will. When his hand distributes charity, it does God's will as though it were literally His hand. When a person puts on *tefillin,* his hand and head function as the servants of the divine will, which desires that *tefillin* should be worn. But when one thinks and speaks words of Torah—meaning that his soul is connected to Torah in the soul's inner garments, its speech and thought—then his connection to the divine will is even more profound" (*Learning from the Tanya,* p. 198).

When we study Scripture, God studies with us p. 152

"When a person performs a commandment, he is like a worker constructing the building. But when a person studies Torah, he is involved with the building plans themselves. He is, so to speak, considering the instructions anew together with the Architect himself. The person performing the commandment is in the action stage, but the person studying Torah is in the planning stage. And at the planning stage, the connection with the planner, with the one who has the will, is deeper and more intimate than it is at the action stage" (*Learning from the Tanya,* p. 199).

Why does God want us to study? p. 153

"Whenever [a person] studies Torah, on whatever level, he becomes one with the divine will. Then, together with God, he contemplates and creates the structure of the world. This participation can take place at any level, high or low. Even when a small boy reads 'In the beginning' with difficulty, he experiences a point of identification with the divine will. Merely by pronouncing these first letters of the Torah, as long as he says them with the proper intent, he is on the same level with the wisest of men; although he does not understand every level of meaning, what he does understand is completely true" (*Learning from the Tanya,* p. 203).

Chapter 17: The Mitzvot: *Understanding God's Commandments*

Whoever grabs hold can reach the other side p. 155

"The performance of a commandment is man's connection to eternity, his entrance into the realm that transcends time. . . . When a person performs a commandment, he is united with *Ein Sof,* and that cannot be erased, even if he leaves the commandment the next moment. The *mitzvah* is a bridge between our world and the Infinite. Therefore, when a person performs a *mitzvah,* he becomes unified with the Infinite. When a person leaves the boundaries of time and space, he leaves limitations behind; he is connected to *Ein Sof* (the Infinite, blessed be He). In this sense, every commandment, whether great or small, is the moment of contact with *Ein Sof;* and that is equal to life itself" (*Learning from the Tanya,* p. 260).

The performance of the *mitzvah* may lie beyond one's understanding p. 156

"The divine wisdom cannot be attained by contemplating abstract truths. Such contemplation yields, at best, false visions, and in other cases, self-images and self-deception. Apprehending the truth of God's wisdom, if only a tiny grain of truth on any particular level—practical or theoretical—is possible only through the comprehension of Torah. The laws that have been spelled out to us in the Torah are that aspect of its divine wisdom that is humanly attainable. When a person comprehends a teaching of Torah, even if it is not an inspirational teaching, it is an articulation of absolute truth, a point of divine wisdom related to a particular problem" (*Opening the Tanya,* p. 147).

Carrying out the commandments p. 157

"When a person performs a commandment in this world, he clothes the inner core of the highest will in the worlds. He is giving the heavenly will a forum in which to appear in this world. At that moment, the divine desire expresses itself within the person performing the commandments and is drawn into the world in which the commandment is being performed. In a sense, a person's body is his soul's garment. Every physical limb is a tool that serves a function of the soul: the eye 'clothes' the power of sight; the ear 'clothes' the ability to hear; the foot 'clothes' the soul's ability to walk; and so forth" (*Learning from the Tanya,* p. 195).

Every *mitzvah* is a part of a whole p. 157

"Indeed, seen as separate and unrelated commandments, each as an individual obligation and burden, these ancillary *mitzvot* seem to be a vast and even an absurd assortment of petty details which are, if not downright intimidating, then at the least troublesome. What we call details, however, are only part of greater units which in turn combined in various ways into a single entity. It is as though in examining the leaves and flowers of a tree, one were to be overwhelmed by the abundance, the variety, and the complexity of detail; but when one realizes that it is all part of the same single growth, all part of the same branching out into manifold forms of the one tree, then the details would cease to be disturbing and would be accepted as intrinsic to the wondrousness of the whole" (*The Thirteen Petalled Rose,* p. 113).

Every *mitzvah* is important p. 158

"With his particular action, a person changes only a small part of reality. When he waves the *lulav* and *etrog,* he cannot transform all of the *etrogim* in the world into *etrogim* used for a *mitzvah,* nor, when he writes a Torah scroll, can he transform all of the animal hides in the world into holy parchment—and there is no need for him to do so. Everything in the world is connected to everything else. Every detail is intermeshed with other details. Every action has an ongoing ripple effect. When a person changes just one particular, he improves the entire world. . . . The purpose of a *mitzvah* is ultimately to elevate the entire world, to completely change the essential meaning of existence in general" (*Understanding the Tanya,* pp. 255–256).

Good and bad deeds do not cancel each other out p. 159

"In Judaism, man is conceived, in all the power of his body and soul, as the central agent, the chief actor on a cosmic stage; he functions, or performs, as a prime mover of worlds, being made in the image of the Creator. Everything he does constitutes an act of creation, both in his own life and in other worlds hidden from sight" (*The Thirteen Petalled Rose,* p. 114).

The importance of intention p. 159

"Every single particle of his body and every nuance of his thought and feeling are connected with forces of all kinds in the cosmos, forces without number; so that the more conscious he is of this order of things, the more significantly does he function as a Jewish person" (*The Thirteen Petalled Rose,* p. 115).

The strength and capacity of a *mitzvah* depend on the life force one puts into it p. 160

"On one occasion, Rabbi Levi Yitzchak conducted a search for someone to blow the shofar on Rosh Hashanah. A number of men demonstrated their knowledge of the mystical meditations that are supposed to enhance shofar blowing, but he was not satisfied.

"One day, a simple man came, and when Rabbi Levi Yitzchak asked him what he would have in mind when he blew the shofar, the man told him, 'Rabbi, I have four daughters of marriageable age. When I blow the shofar, I will think, "Master of the world, I do Your will and blow the shofar, so please do my will and help me marry off my daughters."'

"Rabbi Levi Yitzchak stood up and said, 'You will blow the shofar in my synagogue!'

"Of prime importance in a person's intention is not his intellectual level, knowledge, or even spiritual preparedness but the degree of his intensity as he performs the *mitzvah.* That makes all the difference.

"In short, intent without a *mitzvah* is nothing, but a *mitzvah* without intent, even if it be meager, is still significant. Performing a *mitzvah* for its own sake is the starting point. But when we combine intent with a *mitzvah,* we can arrive at great things.

"The *mitzvah* is a sort of code, a specific, definite message, and the intention is the amplifier" (*Understanding the Tanya,* p. 248).

The three parts of a *mitzvah* p. 161

"When a person's mind grasps and enclothes a concept of Torah, his mind is simultaneously enclothed within the concept. His mind envelops the divine wisdom, and the divine wisdom envelops his mind. The divine wisdom becomes part of him, and he becomes part of it" (*Opening the Tanya,* p. 148).

A higher level of functioning p. 161

"When a person does someone's will, he does not have to understand it. And so the relationship created by his action does not have to break through the obstacles that exist in the relationships based on comprehension. The only question is whether or not he has done that person's will" (*Understanding the Tanya,* p. 245).

The conservation of spiritual essences p. 162

"The person who performs *a mitzvah,* who prays or directs his mind toward the Divine, in doing so creates an angel, which is a sort of reaching out on the part of man to the higher worlds. Such an angel, however, connected in its essence to the man who created it, still lives, on the whole, in a different dimension of being" (*The Thirteen Petalled Rose,* p. 7).

With so much discussion about spiritual matters, it is easy to conclude mistakenly that the spiritual is superior to the material. Rabbi Steinsaltz clarifies this: "Another, more inward aspect is connected with the view that the material world is not inferior, that matter in itself is not lower or worse, and that in a sense the physical world may even be considered the height of

Creation. It is the marvel of Creation for the paradoxical reason that the very existence of matter is a condition that seems to obscure the Divine, and thus could only be the result of a special intention on the part of the Infinite. Matter is a sort of standing wave between the manifestation of God and the hiddenness of God; it is defined by its limitations. To retain its separate and independent existence, infinite force has to be exerted on every particle" (*The Thirteen Petalled Rose,* p. 69).

All the *mitzvot* together form a symphonic whole p. 163

"The system of the *mitzvot* constitutes the design for a coherent harmony, its separate components being like the instruments of an orchestra. So vast is the harmony to be created by this orchestra that it includes the whole world and promises the perfecting of the world" (*The Thirteen Petalled Rose,* p. 115).

Following the Code of Law is not enough p. 164

"In general, there are no preconceptions about what is the correct conduct for all situations, since the correctness of a way of being is itself only measurable in terms of a specific set of circumstances that may or may not recur. There is therefore no possibility of fixing a single standard of behavior. If anything is clear, it is that a rigid, unchanging way is wrong" (*The Thirteen Petalled Rose,* p. 78).

Chapter 18: Kabbalah

As an introductory note to this selection of pebbles, here is the glossary definition of Kabbalah in Rabbi Steinsaltz's multivolume commentary on the *Tanya:*

"Kabbalah is the inner, mystical dimension of the Torah, corresponding to the level of *sod*. As indicated by its name, which means 'what has been received' or 'tradition,' Kabbalah is based on traditions received from one's teachers, who received them, in turn, from their teachers. Kabbalah is not a separate area of Torah knowledge but rather the hidden, spiritual dimension of the revealed aspects of the Torah. Whereas the revealed aspects of the Torah, such as halakhah, speak primarily about visible, physical things, Kabbalah speaks directly about spiritual entities. It speaks of the system of Worlds and *sefirot* through which God creates, sustains, and directs the universe; and it discusses the interaction between those spiritual entities and the performance of *mitzvot* in the physical world. Hence Kabbalah has been called the soul of the Torah. All Torah study is based on the acceptance of tradition and on the principle that because the Torah is a divine gift, a person must make himself into a proper vessel in order to receive it. In the study of Kabbalah, however, these approaches are even more important. Because Kabbalah is the inner spiritual dimension of the Torah, the individual must study it in a way that engages his inner, spiritual dimension. A person who wishes to study Kabbalah should already have an inner understanding of the ideas, and he must pursue the study of Kabbalah in a spirit of purity and holiness, in order to become a suitable vessel" (*Opening the Tanya,* p. 304).

Some books of Jewish history denied the existence of Kabbalah p. 165

As recorded in my book *On the Road with Rabbi Steinsaltz,* the Rabbi expands on this pebble: "People were advised to keep away from subjects they did not know enough about. A little knowledge is dangerous in any field. Since the Torah is a live wire connecting us with God, anyone who gets involved with it without taking precautionary measures run the risk of being electrocuted.

"At a certain point, I would say in the seventeenth century, the religious authorities believed that there was a significant danger. Important books of Kabbalah gathered dust. In Europe, only mature students were permitted to study Kabbalah. In the nineteenth century, authors of the most important books of Jewish history were fiercely antagonistic to Kabbalah, sometimes even denying its existence. It is only in our own time that Kabbalah is beginning to emerge from the obscurity into which it was thrust by enlightened rationalism" (pp. 126–127).

Hasidism is a form of applied Kabbalah p. 166

To round out the impression of this pebble, Rabbi Steinsaltz points out, "Since the time of the expulsion from Spain, the theology of our people is the theology of Kabbalah. Kabbalah permeates every aspect of Judaism. Esoteric wisdom is the basic ingredient of Scripture, of our ritual, and of prayer. The history is not always known accurately. Kabbalah is accepted not only in the Hasidic world but also by people who opposed the Hasidim. The Vilna Gaon was possibly more deeply involved with Kabbalah than many of the Hasidic masters put together" (*On the Road with Rabbi Steinsaltz,* pp. 123–124).

The official theology of the Jewish people p. 166

When Rabbi Steinsaltz delivered the keynote of an annual gathering of the New York Board of Rabbis, he began by saying to the congregational rabbis in attendance, "Kabbalah is the official theology of the Jewish people. In a way, if you are not learning it, if you are not teaching it, I suppose one could question whether or not you are doing your job" (*On the Road with Rabbi Steinsaltz,* p. 122).

Kabbalah and Talmud: different forms of the same thing p. 167

Rabbi Steinsaltz continues with a part of this pebble: "The commonly held view, that Kabbalah and Talmud are in and about different worlds, is a misconception. It is simply not true. There is an organic unity of the whole. The Kabbalah and the Talmud are different forms of expression of the same thing, but each in its own way. There was never a real separation between the daily obligations that we do and the esoteric or mystical aspects of the tradition. They have always been connected. They are different aspects of the same thing. There was never a separation of any real consequence between Kabbalah and the Talmud. They have always been connected" (*On the Road with Rabbi Steinsaltz,* p. 161).

The greatest of the Jewish authorities were immersed in the world of Kabbalah p. 168

"Though the Kabbalah is probably the only extant Jewish theological system, there are various attitudes to its study which question not the relative value of studying Kabbalah, but the qualifications necessary to undertake it" (*Teshuvah,* p. 93).

Kabbalah needs more than a smattering of knowledge p. 169

"There are people in America, in Israel, and in the other countries who are selling Kabbalah. My low regard for this organization is one thing. But it goes much deeper. It is part of the interest in black magic. They take out of Kabbalah every part that has anything to do with obligation. I would call it freewheeling Kabbalah. These Kabbalah centers sell images of power without any obligation, without any future" (*On the Road with Rabbi Steinsaltz,* p. 171).

We study the secret lore but don't see angels p. 169

This selection of pebbles on Kabbalah concludes with this note from Rabbi Steinsaltz: "While recent rabbinic authorities have ruled that study of 'the doctrine of hidden things' need not be suppressed, it is nonetheless advisable to avoid getting into mysticism in an unbalanced way. One drawn to Judaism along the mystical path should take special pains to study halakhah as well, particularly the Talmud and its commentaries, both in order to better understand the Kabbalah itself—a connection a number of well-known scholars have underscored—and in order to keep one's balance and avoid going astray. It is false and misleading to view the Jewish mystical tradition apart from the larger context of Judaism as a whole" (*Teshuvah,* p. 93).

PART V: THE TRIALS OF LIFE

Chapter 19: Struggles, Battles, and Trials

Climbing from level to level p. 173

Connected to the end of this pebble: "The holy is that which is out of bounds, untouchable, and altogether beyond grasp; it cannot be understood or even defined, being so totally unlike anything else. To be holy is to be distinctly other" (*The Thirteen Petalled Rose,* p. 51).

Everyone experiences setbacks p. 174

"Divine service in the world is divided up, with each human being, like the primordial Adam, put in charge of a certain portion of God's garden, to work it and keep it" (*The Thirteen Petalled Rose,* p. 76).

To fall is a sign that one is making progress p. 175

"The very concept of the Divine as infinite implies an activity that is endless, of which one must never grow weary" (*The Thirteen Petalled Rose,* p. 98).

In the Jewish way of life, the challenge is constant p. 175

"It is a continuous going, a going after God a going to God, day after day, year after year" (*The Thirteen Petalled Rose,* p. 99).

The power of repentence p. 175

In a remarkable passage about the power of Torah in *Understanding the Tanya,* Rabbi Steinsaltz again refers to Rabbi Levi Yitzchak of Berditchev: "By its nature, the body instructs a person's ability to understand what happens when he serves God, learns Torah, or performs *mitzvot.* That itself makes it possible for him to do so; that itself explains the existence of the fusion of body and soul. If a person were to be aware of what he is accomplishing, he would have no choice but to explode. The fact that he can calmly sit and learn Torah depends on the fact that he is not aware, that a curtain separates his 'I' from his connection to God, the true One besides Whom there is no other. Rabbi Levi Yitzchak of Berditchev is reputed to have said that one strand of *tzitzit* (fringe) on a prayer shawl in Paradise would cause it to go up in flames. Although the divine light is revealed in Paradise, the incomparably greater revelation of divinity within that *tzitzit* would utterly consume it" (p. 203).

A true penitent stands on a higher level p. 176

"It is using the knowledge of the sin of the past and transforming it into such an extraordinary thirst for good that it becomes a divine force. The more a man was sunk in evil, the more anxious he becomes for good" (*The Thirteen Petalled Rose,* p. 101).

The King of Kings is watching our every move p. 176

Elsewhere, also referring to the Code of Jewish Law, the *Shulkhan Arukh,* Rabbi Steinsaltz writes, "By way of analogy, exposure to radiation above a certain intensity can prove fatal. But also a lesser dose is destructive in the long term. Although the person is not immediately killed, a steady process of deterioration begins, from the time of the exposure and onward. Or, to cite another example, some poisons, such as lead, ingested even in the smallest of quantities, can never be removed. Any immediate damage can usually be overcome, but the cumulative effect over time, as more and more of that material enters the body, can be extremely dangerous. In the same way, every nonholy act, even if permitted, even if rectified and elevated to holiness, leaves a mark of profanity. Thus a person can degenerate spiritually merely by doing things that are permitted by the *Shulkhan Arukh*. The steady accumulation of mundane actions is liable to draw him out of the realm of holiness. A decent person who never deliberately commits a sin, who merely allows himself a so-called normal life, can, in the half-hour or afternoon he devoted to activities devoid of holiness, create a mark of profanity in his body that cannot be removed" (*Opening the Tanya,* p. 209).

Straightening out the distortions p. 177

"This world is therefore no longer a true replica or a true projection of the higher worlds. Only in its original state, that of the Garden of Eden, was it structured as a more or less perfect duplication of the physical world and the spiritual worlds. Since then all the worlds, and our world in particular, have become increasingly distorted" (*The Thirteen Petalled Rose,* p. 86).

Prayer is a time of battle between mighty forces p. 177

Readers familiar with the original edition and the latest (2006) edition of *The Thirteen Petalled Rose* should know that the current version, both in English and in Hebrew, includes two additional chapters. One is a lengthy essay called "Prayer."

Prayer is a trial against oneself p. 178

"The Trials of Life," a section of *The Candle of God* by Rabbi Steinsaltz, is a fourteen-chapter exploration of the struggles and trials of life.

The necessity of instability p. 178

In *On the Road with Rabbi Steinsaltz,* I describe a lecture given by Rabbi Steinsaltz in which he "spoke eloquently on the subject of the necessity of instability in order for there to be growth, progress, change. He talked about airplanes and how safe the airplane is as it flies thirty thousand feet in the air. It's not stable when it's taking off, and it's not stable when it's landing. It is during those moments of shifting, of transition, from one realm to another, from the land to flying, from flying to the land, that there is a period of instability.

"The instability is an essential part of the growth" (*On the Road with Rabbi Steinsaltz,* p. 172).

Tying the broken cord p. 179

See also the essay "Ecclesiastes" by Rabbi Steinsaltz in *On Being Free.*

Chapter 20: Suffering

Bless God for the evil as well as the good p. 181

Elsewhere, Rabbi Steinsaltz retells this story and adds, "This same Rabbi Zusha was once reduced to such poverty as to lack bread, and when he was very hungry, he turned to God and said: 'Master of the Universe! Thank you for giving me an appetite'" (*Opening the Tanya,* p. 283).

Thanking God for suffering is easier said than done p. 182

"Hasidism has adopted a strong stance toward the understanding of divine providence: everything, to the most microscopic level, is under God's direct control. And in this context, the question of accepting suffering with joy and the meaning of evil takes on additional force" (*Learning from the Tanya*, p. 280).

Everything is for the best p. 183

The famous tale regarding Rabbi Akiva is from the Talmud, *Berachot 60b.*

Suffering is a test p. 184

"The reason for the descent of the soul to earthly existence is to experience the trials of life. The soul of man has to be strengthened by test, ordeal, and confrontation with physical reality" (*The Candle of God,* p. 261).

It is a privilege to weep before Him p. 185

Part of the observance of the saddest day in the Jewish yearly cycle, Tisha b'Av (the ninth day of the Hebrew month of Av) is the reading of the book of Lamentations. On Tisha b'Av each year, the Jewish people recall the many painful times that have confronted us and challenged our faith.

God needs your particular pains p. 186

"The trials and severities of a human life are thus not accidental and unfortunate contingencies that simply have to be endured. They are part of the very purpose of a life. In between, there are periods of rest and relaxation, and these provide the strength to stand up to the trials. The ultimate purpose of it all, however, is to know God within" (*The Candle of God,* p. 261).

It is often necessary to pass through some crisis or tragic experience p. 186

This pebble, ironically, brings to mind the following passage: "There are bitter evils and there are sweet evils. In this sense, the trials of life are of all sorts, such as the test of poverty and the test of riches. In which case, a trial experience could be a relatively pleasant affair, a relatively painless procedure, so to speak, but in terms of being tested, the standards are just as rigid" (*The Candle of God,* p. 297).

The only world in which Creation makes sense p. 187

Rabbi Steinsaltz has said, "I am an optimistic Jew, yet with a Jewish definition of optimism. In the eighteenth century, there was a great dispute between Leibniz and Voltaire concerning the type of world that we live in. Leibniz claimed that we live in the best possible world. Voltaire, in *Candide,* reached an opposite conclusion: we live in the worst possible world. In my opinion, the Jewish response to this dispute is as follows: we live in the worst possible world in which there is still hope."

The more pure a man is, the more he is tempted p. 188

"In a sense, the 'righteous person who experiences good' (in the Talmud's phrase) is a person who is immune to evil. He sees things differently than we generally do; he sees not what he lacks but what he has. This is a different spiritual construct, a different way of living, a state of being in which it is impossible to suffer. This is not to say that, in an objective sense, such a person does not experience troubles and ills but that he does not suffer. Rabbi Nachman of Bratslav, certainly not a naive man, suffered from tuberculosis at the end of his life. He never complained about having contracted this disease but expressed great pleasure if, between coughing and spitting up blood, he was able to say a few words" (*Opening the Tanya,* p. 285).

Rabbi Steinsaltz is clear. The tests and trials of life are of Divine origin and can be reframed to be apprehended as gifts from above: "We receive gifts from heaven, and they are always positive, even though at first glance, that is not always apparent. Sometimes we must give them a second or even a third look before we are able to learn how to relate to them as gifts from God. Although this explanation does not solve a person's pain, it removes his sadness. Although it does not resolve the problems, it removes his worries. The sadness that a person feels comes from his perception that God has treated him unfairly, and that feeling must be eliminated. A person can do so when he sees suffering not as a punishment but as a reward—even if it is hard to accept and even if it takes some time to learn how to relate to it. Worry comes from thinking, *What will the future bring? What if it will be even worse?* This question can be resolved when one realizes that the good will not necessarily be revealed immediately; it may, in fact, never be revealed, for some gifts appear good and others simply not" (*Learning from the Tanya,* pp. 288–289).

The wholeness of a broken heart p. 189

This image, of the wholeness of a broken heart, is usually attributed to Rabbi Menachem Mendel of Kotzk.

Understanding the difference between pain and sadness p. 189

Pages 280–290 in *Learning from the Tanya* focus on suffering.

A strategy to banish sadness p. 190

"In itself, and even when used for holy purposes, sadness is not healthy. But at times, it must be used, just as a pathogen may be used, to effect an extreme reaction" (*Learning from the Tanya,* p. 270).

The worst possible world where there is still hope p. 190

The comment earlier in the Notes for this chapter, under, "The only world in which Creation makes sense," apply here also.

In the struggle of existence, one discovers the harmony p. 191

"The trial experience is thus a process through which a person reaches a higher level of being and of knowledge" (*The Candle of God,* p. 322).

The joys of the next world p. 192

"Evil does not act independently but is always an instrument for good. In a broader sense, 'evil defines good' (*Sefer Yitzirah*). Evil indicates where good ends; thus, through evil, good can be recognized clearly. In this sense, everything evil is a tool that we can use to reach goals that are good. According to this understanding, any seeming victory of evil is only a way station on the road toward good. Every descent is a 'descent for the purpose of ascent.' Evil is one of the tools of universal good; it is the pedestal, the base on which all good stands on display" (*Learning from the Tanya,* pp. 280–281).

Chapter 21: Evil

Understanding evil p. 193

The terms Rabbi Steinsaltz uses to explore the subject of evil are from Kabbalistic tradition, like *kelipah* ("husk") and *sitra achra* ("the other side"). In the first chapter of *Opening the Tanya,* pages 58–60, Rabbi Steinsaltz defines these terms.

Evil is a parasite p. 194

"Forces of evil that had parasitically attached themselves to a person are not easily compelled to act in the direction of the good" (*The Thirteen Petalled Rose,* p. 102).

Evil must be fought p. 195

See Rabbi Steinsaltz's essay "Good vs. Evil" at http://www.steinsaltz.org. Rabbi Steinsaltz writes, "Educating people on how to cope with evil is one element that is sorely missing in our pedagogy system. So many refuse to even admit to the existence of the dark side. Knowledge and awareness of the existence of evil should be a required element of both public and private education, from preschool to adulthood.

"While we all may yearn for nothing but sweetness and light in our lives, we will always find one bully trying to beat others down—or, on a broader scale, a dictator willing to kill others to attain his own goals, or a terrorist who believes that the road to heaven is paved with corpses. Raising awareness of evil is not education for pessimism or for the notion of all-present evil. Human beings and societies, generally, have many positive aspects as well, and they must not be ignored.

"It is a simple fact of life that most people have more good in them than evil. Even on the national and international level, there are many good intentions for solving the very real needs and problems of the world.

"The best way to combat evil is to promote good. This, too, cannot be accomplished by ignoring evil. The battle requires an enormous commitment on our part. We cannot simply sit and wait for a good angel to intervene.

"There is nothing wrong with believing that guardian angels keep an eye on us, but we must remember that ultimately we are responsible for most of the work—and from time to time, we can accept a little assistance from the angels."

The struggle with the evil inclination p. 197

Chapter 30 in *Understanding the Tanya* explores this subject.

After one has defeated the evil impulse, it ceases to have any meaning p. 198

"The complete correction of past evil cannot be brought about merely by acknowledgment of wrong and contrition; indeed, this acknowledgment often leads, in practice, to a loss of incentive, a state of passivity, of depression; furthermore, the very preoccupation with memories of an evil impulse may well revive that impulse's hold on a person" (*The Thirteen Petalled Rose,* p. 101).

No two people are alike in their susceptibility to temptation p. 198

"Some lives have an emotional emphasis; others, an intellectual; for some the way of joy is natural; for others existence is full of effort and struggle; there are people for whom purity of heart is the most difficult thing in the world, while for others it is given as a gift from birth" (*The Thirteen Petalled Rose,* p. 102).

Our thoughts give birth to demons p. 199

"For beside its visibly destructive consequences, every act of malice or evil creates an abstract gnostic being, who is a bad angel, an angel belonging to the plane of evil corresponding to this state of mind that brought it into being. In their inner essence, however, the creatures of realms of evil are not independent entities living by their own forces; their existence is contingent on our world" (*The Thirteen Petalled Rose,* p. 20).

Transforming evil into good p. 199

"The penitent thus does more than return to his proper place. He performs an act of amendment of cosmic significance; he restores the sparks of holiness which had been captured by the powers of evil. The sparks that he had dragged down and attached himself are now raised up with him, and a host of forces of evil return and are transformed into forces of good" (*The Thirteen Petalled Rose,* p. 102).

Developing the capacity to bless evil as well as good p. 200

"The *Tanya* offers an additional, more profound explanation. That which appears evil, the author explains, is not essentially evil but a good that we cannot see. Although certain events may appear to be evil, this does not express their essential character but only reflects our insufficient understanding" (*Learning from the Tanya,* p. 281).

PART VI: GUIDANCE

Chapter 22: Learning and Teaching

Freeing the mind of worry p. 203

Also about Elijah, commenting on the statement by Hillel in the Talmud "Be of the disciples of Aaron, loving peace and pursuing peace, loving the creatures and drawing them near to the Torah," Rabbi Steinsaltz writes, "Hillel the Elder is not observing that we must love the righteous, but 'creatures.' *Creatures* is a general term that refers to all beings, even the very lowest, of whom we can say nothing more positive than that they were created.

"In this regard, the prophet Elijah was once asked why God created rodents and other crawling creatures. He replied that when God looks at His world and sees the evil of human beings and wishes to destroy them, He considers those rodents as well and decides that—just as He allows them to exist—so will he allow such people to exist. . . .

"There are people whose only saving grace is that there are other creatures even lower than they. It is of such people that Hillel the Elder tells us that it is a *mitzvah* to love them and bring them close to Torah" (*Understanding the Tanya,* p. 132).

One must investigate each matter specifically p. 204

"As a fundamental approach, Judaism has been able to develop two branches, which, from the outside, seem to be worlds apart and totally contradictory: the soaring power of prophecy and the careful performing of the *mitzvot* with precise attention to detail" (*The Thirteen Petalled Rose,* p. 80).

There is always more than one viewpoint p. 204

"In certain societies and cultures, love, pity, compassion may be considered good; and yet there may also be occasions, outside these cultures and even within them, when these qualities could be considered bad, leading one astray into sadness or sin. Similarly, pride, selfishness, and even hate are not always bad attributes" (*The Thirteen Petalled Rose,* p. 77).

One may forget what was known, but the impression cannot be effaced p. 205

Rabbi Steinsaltz tells the following story about memory in *Understanding the Tanya:* "Once a Hasidic rebbe and his student, a distinguished Torah scholar, had differing recollections of a statement in the *Tosafot* commentary. Although the scholar had seen that passage just a few days before, the rebbe said, 'I have not seen it for fifteen years, yet I am certain that I am right.' When he was proved correct, the abashed scholar asked him how he could remember so well.

"The rebbe asked him, 'Do you remember your wedding?'

" 'Certainly,' he said.

" 'Do you recall who accompanied you to the canopy, who stood to your right, and who veiled the bride?'

" 'Of course.'

" 'For me,' the rebbe said, 'every time I learn Torah is like a wedding.' "

He adds, "A great rabbi with a flawless memory was once asked how it is that he never forgot. He replied, 'How is it that people do not forget to put food in their mouths? When a person's life depends on something, he does not forget it' " (p. 253).

It may be sufficient for each person to know as much as he can absorb p. 206

"In spite of all the bonds uniting the individual soul either with a higher source or with every other soul, each particular spark, each individual soul, is unique and special, in terms of its essence, its capacity, and what is demanded of it. No two souls coincide in their actions, their functions, and their paths. No one soul can take the place of another, and even the greatest of the great cannot fill the special role, the particular place, of another that may be the smallest of the small" (*The Thirteen Petalled Rose,* p. 38).

The sin of an uneducated person is considered unintentional p. 206

See the Talmud, *Bava Metzia* 33b.

The degree of guilt is proportional to one's level of knowledge p. 207

Bava Metzia 33b is also relevant to this pebble.

I'm interested in almost everything p. 208

In response to a journalist, Rabbi Steinsaltz once said, "Generally speaking, I would say that my turning to religion came about because of two reasons that may not be considered religious enough. One was that I am, by nature, an unbeliever, which means that I couldn't take lots of things for granted that other people could. I discovered when I was very young that people do believe in lots of things. People were ardently religious because they were taken in by things that other people say, things that people assume to be true. Now, being an unbeliever almost by nature, I couldn't believe them, so I began to ask questions—but not questions just to annoy people. My first name, Adin, means 'gentle.' Someone with this name is almost fated to be very rude. I was always a delicate boy, so people used to come and pat my head, and say, 'It's such a nice name. It suits you so well.' So of course, when you hear this so many times, you become coarser and coarser and more and more rude. I didn't want to annoy people. But I began asking questions, many questions about things that were accepted in Israel and in other places. I was perhaps a greater nonbeliever than the rest of my countrymen. They were such great nonbelievers that they didn't even believe in Judaism. I was such a nonbeliever that I didn't even believe in heresy. So this was the turning, a very important one. I discovered that one has to believe in many heresies in order to be a heretic. But in order to accept heresy, one has to be a believer. And if you have to be a believer, it becomes a matter of choice in what to believe. That was one point. The other point was that, as a boy, and certainly as a young man, I was full of desires. Big ones. And the world didn't seem big enough. I wanted more and more and still more. In a certain way, this was a turn into a fourth dimension, or a fifth dimension, or whatever dimension. My turning toward religious thinking or thinking about something like God came because the world was too small. Because of this, because I felt that unless a person becomes attached to the Infinite, the world becomes far too restrictive to live in. My turnabout was a very slow one, a very painful one. I'm still trying to become better."

A true leader can be understood by everyone p. 209

Also from Rabbi Steinsaltz on the Maggid of Mezritch: "As stated in *Avot,* 'Do not be like servants who serve the master in order to receive a reward, but like servants who serve the master not for the sake of receiving a reward.' For most of his life, the Maggid of Mezheritch lived in terrible poverty. When conditions grew especially difficult, his wife groaned, and, hearing her, the Maggid groaned as well. At that moment, he heard a proclamation in heaven that he had lost his portion in the world to come, because a person of his stature should not have descended to such a level. Joyously, the Maggid exclaimed, 'Now I can serve God in truth, without any desire to receive a reward!'" (*Learning from the Tanya,* p. 128).

The study of science p. 209

"Philosophy, psychology, science, all merely isolate the basic problem within an observable small field where it can in turn be broken down into secondary problems, every one of which may, by itself, be important and certainly interesting but, taken together, nevertheless seem far removed from any truly satisfactory response" (*The Thirteen Petalled Rose,* p. 104).

I have always been suspicious of artificial means—such as mantras or drugs p. 210

Also of related interest is a brief conversation with Rabbi Steinsaltz about marijuana. See my book *On the Road with Rabbi Steinsaltz,* pages 37–38.

There are three things that are connected—the Jews with the Torah and the Torah with God p. 211

In *The Thirteen Petalled Rose,* Rabbi Steinsaltz writes, "As someone once aptly summed it up: other religions have a concept of scripture as deriving from Heaven, but only Judaism seems to be based on the idea that the Torah Scripture is itself Heaven" (p. 65).

A good teacher p. 212

"To be sure, a person needs a special teacher" (*The Thirteen Petalled Rose,* p. 78).

When a teacher is a fake, the students know it right away p. 212

There is a section in *On the Road with Rabbi Steinsaltz* called "Finding a Spiritual Guide": "If your teacher is like an angel, then go and receive Torah from him. Of course, we are handicapped in this case because, among other things, we don't know what angels look like, so if I am searching for an angel-like teacher, I may sometimes bump into something which is a very strange image that I have of angels and which is perhaps wrong" (p. 131).

And also, "The person who claims that he knows everything is most possibly a liar. The people who are undertaking to solve all the questions that you have are perhaps confidence men" (p. 132).

A rabbi is one who teaches others p. 214

Talmud, *Avodah Zarah* 17a.

Chapter 23: Spiritual Direction

The emphasis is not on specific qualities but on the right measure p. 217

This is the subject of the chapter "The Way of Choice: An Answer to Ethics" in *The Thirteen Petalled Rose*. For example, "In Hebrew, good attributes are called 'good measures,' which suggests that the excellence of equality is determined by its proportion, not by its being what it is in itself, but by its properly related use in particular circumstances. Everything that is not in the right measure, that relates out of proportion to a situation, tends to be bad" (p. 77).

Real battles of life p. 218

"The sages have been well aware of the many sides of Torah. Whether it is an elixir of life or an elixir of death depends on whether the person who occupies himself with it is pure in heart and is open to receive what it confers" (*In the Beginning,* p. 201).

One has to be constantly on the alert p. 218

In *The Thirteen Petalled Rose,* Rabbi Steinsaltz writes, "It is, nevertheless, a continuous going, and going after God, a going to God, day after day, year after year" (p. 99). And also, "A basic idea underlying Jewish life is that there are no special frameworks for holiness. A man's relation to God is not set apart on a higher plane, not relegated to some special corner of time and place with all the rest of life taking place somewhere else. The Jewish attitude is that life in all its aspects, in its totality, must somehow or other be bound up with holiness" (p. 114).

One must learn the truth p. 219

"According to tradition there are said to be six hundred and thirteen commandments in the Torah. This, however, is misleading in a number of respects. For one thing, many of the positive commandments—that is, *mitzvot* that obligate one to perform certain actions—along with many of the prohibitions, are not actually concerned with life but refer either to the general structure of the whole of the Torah or to the Jewish nation as a body. No Jew, therefore, can expect to keep all of the *mitzvot*. Actually, only a small number of the *mitzvot* relate to daily life, though if one adds to the formal list of *mitzvot* all the minute details that are not specifically included, one arrives at a sum of not hundreds but thousands of things that are to be done at certain times and certain places and in a special way" (*The Thirteen Petalled Rose*, p. 113).

Living for the sake of Heaven p. 219

"The possibilities of relating and responding to God are countless in number. There is no above or below in approaching Him" (*The Thirteen Petalled Rose*, p. 81).

Only through the body and the physical world can the genuinely spiritual be achieved p. 220

"In Judaism, man is conceived, in all the power of his body and soul, as the central agent, the chief actor on a cosmic stage; he functions, or performs, as a prime mover of worlds, being made in the image of the Creator. Everything he does constitutes an act of creation, both in his own life and in other worlds hidden from his sight. Every single particle of his body and every nuance of his thought and feeling are connected with forces of all kinds in the cosmos, forces without number; so that the more conscious he is of this order of things, the more significantly does he function as a Jewish person" (*The Thirteen Petalled Rose,* p. 114).

Avoiding idolatry p. 221

"The prohibition simply reiterates the fundamental opposition to idolatry on all its levels" (*The Thirteen Petalled Rose,* p. 83).

Contending with one's imagination p. 222

Regarding Desargues' theorem, Rabbi Steinsaltz said, "Once you imagine a point in the infinite, the theorem can be proved. It is the same with our world. To begin to understand, we must imagine the infinite" (*On the Road with Rabbi Steinsaltz,* p. 113).

The pitfalls of success p. 223

"Repentance also includes the expectance of a response, of a confirmation from God that this is indeed the way, that this is the direction. Nevertheless, the essence of repentance is bound up more with turning than with response. When response is direct and immediate, the process of repentance cannot continue, because it has in a way arrived at its goal" (*The Thirteen Petalled Rose,* p. 97).

The sincere worshiper of God has to tighten the tension p. 223

"One of its essential components (repentance) is an increase of tension, the tension of the ongoing experience and of yearning" (*The Thirteen Petalled Rose,* p. 97).

A better wine is far more difficult to appreciate p. 224

"The greater the test, the more meaningful the overcoming of the ordeal. As a result, the person can rise to a higher level" (*In the Beginning,* p. 303).

This is exactly the time when one must not sleep p. 224

"The very concept of the Divine as infinite implies an activity that is endless, of which one must never grow weary" (*The Thirteen Petalled Rose,* p. 98).

GLOSSARY

Ahavat Yisrael Love of Israel, the Jewish people.

Al Chet "For the sin"; confessional prayer on Yom Kippur.

Baal haTanya Rabbi Schneur Zalman of Liadi, author of the *Tanya.*

Baal Shem Tov Founder of the Hasidic movement.

Baal teshuvah "One who has returned"; a person who has returned to God.

Bava Metzia "Middle Gate," a tractate of the Talmud.

Chayah One of the five levels of the soul.

Chesed The *sefirah* of loving-kindness.

Chevrusa Torah study partner.

Chokhmah The *sefirah* of wisdom.

Chutzpah Yiddish for audacity.

Dybbuk A wandering soul that enters a person's body.

Ein Sof "Without end"; a name for God emphasizing God's infinity.

***Etrog* (pl., *etrogim*)** A citrus fruit used in the ritual observance of Sukkot.

Gam zu l'tova "Also this is good"; expression that everything is for good.

Gan Eden The Garden of Eden.

Gevurah The *sefirah* of restraint and contraction.

Haggadah The book containing the story and ritual for the Passover seder.

Halakhah Jewish law.

Hasid (pl., Hasidim) "Pious one"; one who identifies with the Hasidic movement.

Hillel Talmudic sage from the first century B.C.E.

Hillel Zeitlin Yiddish and Hebrew writer of the late nineteenth and early twentieth centuries.

Kabbalah From the root "to receive," the spiritual theology of the Jewish people.

***Kavvanah* (pl., *kavvanot*)** Inner intention and focus on God.

***Kelipah* (pl., *kelipot*)** "Husk"; Kabbalistic term for anything that is unholy or obscures the Divine.

Lechah Dodi Kabbalistic poem from the sixteenth century that is now part of the liturgy.

Lulav Palm branch used in the ritual of Sukkot.

Ma'asim tovim Good deeds.

Maggid An especially gifted preacher, able to reach everyone.

Maggid of Mezritch Disciple and successor to the Baal Shem Tov.

Malkhut The *sefirah* of kingdom, also a symbol of the Sabbath.

Mensch An honest, decent person.

Merkavah Literally, "chariot," a Kabbalistic term for a thing, person, or spiritual entity that is completely obedient to the Divine will.

Midrash A major branch of the Oral Torah consisting largely of homiletic and legal material. One item from this literature is called a *midrash* (pl., *midrashim*).

***Mitzvah* (pl., *mitzvot*)** A Divine commandment.

Nefesh One of the five levels of the soul.

Neshamah One of the five levels of the soul.

Oneg "Delight."

Passover Jewish holy days commemorating the Exodus from Egypt.

Pharaoh Ruler of ancient Egypt.

Pirkei Avot "Chapters of the Fathers," a section of the Oral Torah.

Rabban Yochanan ben Zakkai First-century Jewish sage.

Rabbi Akiva Jewish sage of the late first and early second centuries.

Rabbi Chaim Vital Disciple of the great Kabbalist, Rabbi Isaac Luria.

Rabbi Isaac Luria Sixteenth-century rabbi, recognized as the greatest Kabbalist in history.

Rabbi Joseph Karo Sixteenth-century rabbi and compiler of the Code of Jewish Law.

Rabbi Levi Yitzchak of Berditchev Hasidic leader of the late eighteenth and early nineteenth centuries.

Rabbi Menachem Mendel of Kotzk Nineteenth-century Hasidic leader, known as the Kotzker Rebbe.

Rabbi Nachman of Bratslav Hasidic leader of the late eighteenth and early nineteenth centuries.

Rabbi Schneur Zalman of Liadi Nineteenth-century Hasidic leader, author of the *Tanya.*

Rabbi Shimon bar Yochai First-century Jewish sage, author of the *Zohar.*

Rabbi Simcha Bunim Hasidic master of the early nineteenth century.

Rabbi Zusha of Anipoli Legendary Hasidic teacher.

Rambam (Maimonides) Rabbi Moses ben Maimon, twelfth-century Jewish philosopher and scholar.

Ramban (Nachmanides) Rabbi Moses ben Nachman, twelfth-century Jewish scholar and Kabbalist.

Rashi Eleventh-century Jewish sage and biblical and Talmudic commentator.

Rebbe A Hasidic spiritual leader.

Ruach One of the five levels of the soul.

Seder "Order"; the Passover family home ritual.

Sefer Yitzirah An early Kabbalistic text.

Sefirah **(pl., *sefirot*)** Any of the ten channels of Divine energy, corresponding to the ten attributes of the soul, through which God creates, sustains, and directs the world.

Shabbat The seventh day of Creation, the traditional day of rest.

Shavuot Spring holy festival, commemorating the giving of the Torah.

Shekhinah The presence of God.

Shema Yisrael Jewish prayer, recited at least twice a day, declaring God's unity.

Shivah "Seven"; the seven-day period of mourning observed by Jews after a person's death.

Shulkhan Arukh "Prepared Table"; the authoritative Code of Jewish Law.

sitra achra "The other side," a general term for evil.

Sukkot Fall harvest festival, commemorating the wandering of the Jews in the desert.

talmid chakham "Student of the wise"; honorific title for a Jewish scholar.

Talmud The written form of the Oral Torah.

Tanya Kabbalistic text by Rabbi Schneur Zalman of Liadi.

Tefillah Prayer.

Tefillin Small cases containing scriptural passages written on parchment that are worn during prayer.

Teshuvah "Repentence," a return to a God.

Tikkun Leil Shavuot The order customarily recited during the all-night Torah study on the holy day of Shavuot.

Tikkun olam "Repair of the world"; a person's work in the world.

Tisha b'Av Day of mourning recalling the destruction of the Temple in Jerusalem.

Torah The Five Books of Moses, or Jewish religious studies in general.

***Tzaddik* (pl., *tzaddikim*)** A saint; a righteous person.

Tzedakah "Justice"; the Hebrew word for charity.

Tzemach Tzedek Nineteenth-century Hasidic leader.

Tzimtzum "Contraction"; Kabbalistic term for God's making room for Creation.

Tzitzit Fringes on the end of a Jewish prayer shawl.

Vilna Gaon (Gaon of Vilna) The eighteenth-century leader of Lithuanian Jewry.

Yechidah One of the five levels of the soul.

Yeshiva A school dedicated to Torah study.

Yom Kippur The Day of Atonement.

Yom tov General term for a holy day.

Zohar Major Kabbalistic text.

BIBLIOGRAPHY

The following books by Rabbi Adin Steinsaltz are available in English.

Biblical Images (Jason Aronson, 1994)

The Candle of God: Discourses on Chasidic Thought (Jason Aronson, 1999)

A Dear Son to Me: A Collection of Speeches and Articles (Israel Institute for Talmudic Publications, 2002)

The Essential Talmud, Thirtieth Anniversary Edition (Basic Books, 2006)

A Guide to Jewish Prayer (Schocken, 2002)

In the Beginning: Discourses on Chasidic Thought (Jason Aronson, 1992)

Learning from the Tanya: Volume Two in the Definitive Commentary on the Moral and Mystical Teachings of a Classic Work of Kabbalah (Jossey-Bass, 2005)

The Long Shorter Way: Discourses on Chasidic Thought (Jason Aronson, 1988)

The Miracle of the Seventh Day: A Guide to the Spiritual Meaning, Significance, and Weekly Practice of the Jewish Sabbath (Jossey-Bass, 2003)

On Being Free (Jason Aronson, 1995)

Opening the Tanya: Discovering the Moral and Mystical Teachings of a Classic Work of Kabbalah (Jossey-Bass, 2003)

The Passover Haggadah (Carta, 1983)

The Seven Lights: On the Major Jewish Festivals (Jason Aronson, 2000)

Simple Words: Thinking About What Really Matters in Life (Simon & Schuster, 1999)

The Strife of the Spirit (Jason Aronson, 1988)

The Sustaining Utterance: Discourses on Chasidic Thought (Jason Aronson, 1989)

The Tales of Rabbi Nachman of Bratslav (Jason Aronson, 1993)

Talmudic Images (Jason Aronson, 1997)

Teshuvah: A Guide for the Newly Observant Jew (Jason Aronson, 1996)

The Thirteen Petalled Rose (Basic Books, 1980; expanded edition, 2006)

Understanding the Tanya: Volume Three in the Definitive Commentary on a Classic Work of Kabbalah (Jossey-Bass, 2007)

We Jews: Who Are We and What Should We Do? (Jossey-Bass, 2005)

Rabbi Steinzaltz is also quoted extensively in my own book, *On the Road with Rabbi Steinsaltz: 25 Years of Pre-Dawn Car Trips, Mind-Blowing Encounters, and Inspiring Conversations with a Man of Wisdom* (Jossey-Bass, 2006).

ABOUT RABBI ADIN STEINSALTZ

Rabbi Adin Steinsaltz is a teacher, philosopher, social critic, and prolific author who has been hailed by *Time* magazine as a "once-in-a-millennium scholar." His lifelong work in Jewish education earned him the Israel Prize, that country's highest honor.

Born in Jerusalem in 1937 to secular parents, Rabbi Steinsaltz studied physics and chemistry at the Hebrew University. Following graduation, he established several experimental schools and at the age of twenty-four became Israel's youngest school principal.

In 1965, he began his monumental Hebrew translation and commentary on the Talmud. The rabbi's classic work of Kabbalah, *The Thirteen Petalled Rose,* was first published in 1980 and is now available in eight languages. In all, Rabbi Steinsaltz has written more than sixty books and hundreds of articles on a wide range of subjects.

Continuing his work as a teacher and spiritual mentor, Rabbi Steinsaltz established a network of schools and educational institutions in Israel and the former Soviet Union.

He has served as scholar in residence at the Woodrow Wilson International Center for Scholars in Washington, D.C., and the Institute for Advanced Studies at Princeton

University. His honorary degrees include doctorates from Yeshiva University, Ben Gurion University of the Negev, Bar Ilan University, Brandeis University, and Florida International University.

Rabbi Steinsaltz lives in Jerusalem. He and his wife have three children and ten grandchildren.

ABOUT ARTHUR KURZWEIL

Arthur Kurzweil (http://www.arthurkurzweil.com) is a popular scholar in residence and guest speaker for synagogues and other Jewish organizations across the United States. He is known throughout the world of Jewish books as a prolific author, publisher, and teacher. And as a member of the Society of American Magicians, he regularly performs an entertaining one-person presentation, "Searching for God in a Magic Shop," blending profound Jewish teachings with a number of fascinating illusions.

The author of the best-selling book *From Generation to Generation: How to Trace Your Jewish Genealogy and Family History* (Jossey-Bass, 2004), Arthur Kurzweil is a recipient of the Lifetime Achievement Award from the International Association of Jewish Genealogical Societies for his "trailblazing work . . . and continued inspiration" to all Jewish genealogists. He also received the Distinguished Humanitarian Award from the Melton Center for Jewish Studies at Ohio State University for his "unique contribution to Jewish education," and he is on the advisory board of the International Institute for Jewish Genealogy at Hebrew University's Jewish National and University Library in Jerusalem.

Arthur Kurzweil was editor in chief of the Jewish Book Club for seventeen years. He is also a past president of the Jewish

Book Council. For nearly two decades, he was vice president of Jason Aronson Publishers, during which time he published over 650 titles of Jewish interest and distributed more books on Jewish topics than any other single source in the United States.

Arthur Kurzweil is also the author of *Kabbalah for Dummies* (Wiley, 2007) and *The Torah for Dummies* (Wiley, 2008).

His previous book devoted to Rabbi Steinsaltz is *On the Road with Rabbi Steinsaltz: 25 Years of Pre-Dawn Car Trips, Mind-Blowing Encounters, and Inspiring Conversations with a Man of Wisdom* (Jossey-Bass, 2006). Arthur Kurzweil frequently teaches classes using Rabbi Steinsaltz's translations and commentaries on the Talmud and the rabbi's other writings, and he maintains a popular blog on Rabbi Steinsaltz's teachings (http://essentialsteinsaltz.blogspot.com).

INDEX

E

Q

R

Also by Rabbi Adin Steinsaltz

We Jews

Who Are We and What Should We Do?

Rabbi Adin Steinsaltz

Hardcover

ISBN: 978-0-7879-7915-7

Thirteen million Jews throughout the United States and the world are famously divided and contentious about their identity, political position, social role, and spiritual goals. However, if there is one authentic voice of leadership in the Jewish community, it is scholar, teacher, mystic, scientist, and social critic Rabbi Adin Steinsaltz. He is internationally regarded as one of the greatest rabbis of this century and of the last.

In *We Jews*, Rabbi Steinsaltz explores the most important issues that concern Jews today as Jews. He provides wise and uplifting answers to Jews everywhere, whether they are secular and assimilated or orthodox—Are we a nation or a religion? Are the stereotypes of Jews really true? Why are Jews so controversial? How can we navigate the opposing forces of diversity, culture, and politics? Can we survive intermarriage and the loss of tradition? Do we still worship the Golden Calf?

In this book, Rabbi Steinsaltz sees causes and consequences, achievements and failures, looks at the contemporary world, and observes the dreams and longings of modern Jewish people. Written as an intimate and inspiring internal memo to the whole Jewish family, *We Jews* answers these questions and many more in a way that is at once insightful and inspiring.

Opening the Tanya

Discovering the Moral and Mystical Teachings of a Classic Work of Kabbalah

Rabbi Adin Steinsaltz

Hardcover
ISBN: 978-0-7879-6798-7

As relevant today as it was when it was first written more than two hundred years ago, the *Tanya* helps us to see the many thousands of complexities, doubts, and drives within us as expressions of a single basic problem: the struggle between our Godly soul and our animal soul. *Opening the Tanya* is a groundbreaking book that offers a definitive introduction, explanation, and commentary upon the *Tanya.*

The internationally celebrated Rabbi Adin Steinsaltz, who has dedicated his life to the study, teaching, and writing of books that explain Jewish scripture, religious practice, spirituality, and mysticism to Jews and non-Jews throughout the world, is the author of this explanation and line-by-line commentary on the *Tanya.*

Opening the Tanya guides us to achieve harmony of body and soul, of earthliness and transcendence. This remarkable book helps us to learn how we can each elevate our soul to a higher level of awareness and understanding, until our objectives and aspirations are synonymous with our Godly potential.

Understanding the Tanya

Volume Three in the Definitive Commentary on a Classic Work of Kabbalah by the World's Foremost Authority

Rabbi Adin Steinsaltz

Hardcover

ISBN: 978-0-7879-8826-5

"The scope of Steinsaltz's work can only be compared to Rashi's [the great medieval commentator]. He has revolutionized the way the Talmud is studied. His commentaries will live for centuries."

—Washington Post

Understanding the Tanya guides the reader through one of the most extraordinary books of moral teachings ever written. The *Tanya* is a seminal document in both the study of Hasidic thought and of Kabbalah—Jewish mysticism. With a keen understanding of the profound struggles within the human soul, the *Tanya* helps us understand how we can raise ourselves to higher and higher spiritual levels.

The first book in the series, *Opening the Tanya,* introduced us to the "beinoni," that person who is neither inherently righteous nor evil, but who seeks to reach moral perfection even as he struggles with an animal soul. The second volume, *Learning from the Tanya*, offers a deeper description of the moral tensions within each of us. This third volume, *Understanding the Tanya*, continues where volume two left off in its page-by-page commentary on the linear sequence of the *Tanya*'s original text.

Also by Arthur Kurzweil

On the Road with Rabbi Steinsaltz

25 Years of Pre-Dawn Car Trips, Mind-Blowing Encounters, and Inspiring Conversations with a Man of Wisdom

Arthur Kurzweil

Hardcover

ISBN: 978-0-7879-8324-6

Arthur Kurzweil—himself a Jewish scholar, author, teacher, and publisher—has been a disciple of Rabbi Steinsaltz's for over 25 years, as well as the Rabbi's designated chauffer in the United States. While stuck in countless traffic jams and attending the Rabbi's lectures at universities, government agencies, synagogues, and seminars, Arthur Kurzweil has had the rare opportunity of personally learning from his inspired teacher and has become intimately familiar with the Rabbi's wisdom and teachings.

On the Road with Rabbi Steinsaltz presents an intimate portrait of this wise and holy man as he has never been seen before as Kurzweil shares the Rabbi's most personal, humorous, and inspiring tales.

You will feel like a backseat passenger in Arthur's car as he and Rabbi Steinsaltz discuss provocative issues such as:

- How can we develop a personal relationship with God?
- What are some of the sublime ideas contained in Kabbalah?
- Why has God created a world with so much suffering in it?
- Can we be religious and live fully in the world?
- How can we tell what is important and what is unimportant in this life?
- Can we be religious and keep our sense of humor?

Throughout the book Arthur Kurzweil also shares Rabbi Steinsaltz's views and teachings on Jewish identity and the role of Jews in modern society. So grab your overcoat and come along for a ride with Rabbi Steinsaltz and Arthur Kurzweil—a ride that could very well change your life.